PRAISE FOR *BOUNCE FORWARD·* ⁻ *RESILIENCE OF LE⸀*

"I don't know if it's because I'm so interested in this ⸏   ⸌ause the book is so well written or both, but for one of the first times in my life ɪ read this entire manuscript in one sitting. I could not stop turning the pages. Each chapter offered cutting-edge research, concrete examples, tools for self-assessment, and questions for reflection and discussion.

"Elle Allison-Napolitano has written the quintessential book on educational leadership. Grounded in theory, drawn from her own experience, and based on numerous interviews with school leaders, Allison-Napolitano uses cohesive strategies, explicit cases, and an array of inventories designed to help school leaders reflect on their strengths as well as weaknesses.

"Allison-Napolitano establishes a clear framework for improvement as she combines current research from neurobiology, sales management, psychology, sociology, and a number of subject areas to illustrate her points about school leadership and resiliency. Any leader (school or otherwise) will benefit from her informative, easy-to-read narrative along with the myriad of print and digital resources she offers.

"I would recommend this book to any prospective school leaders, those new to the field, and veteran school leaders who want to be renewed. Novice leaders will enjoy the step-by-step model Allison-Napolitano offers for achieving effective leadership. Veteran leaders will appreciate the thought-provoking challenges she offers for self-improvement. Her astute observations are practical as well as inspiring. This is a must-read for every administrator."

—Debbie Silver, Corwin Author
Fall Down 7 Times, Get Up 8 and
Those Who Should, Teach (forthcoming)

"In *Bounce Forward: The Extraordinary Resilience of Leadership,* Elle Allison-Napolitano speaks directly to each reader in a voice full of enthusiasm and spirit. As a result, this book on leadership succeeds where many fail in that it actually provides the energy to go along with its strong content. The numerous leadership stories are part of the secret of this book, but, in addition, it's the way in which Elle sits with the reader and speaks with a voice of experience that never loses its 'bounce.' She has been there, and she truly understands the power and the rewards of resilience in leadership. It's rare to read a book on leadership with a smile on your face even as you learn some powerful lessons from the many activities, questions, and tools provided. This is not only a must-read, it's a must-re-read, and a must-practice, and a must-share. There is no doubt that we can all use a 'bounce forward' as we provide leadership during these difficult times."

—Richard Hanzelka, PhD, Professor of Education
St. Ambrose University
Davenport, IA
Past President of ASCD

"Public education's 21st century leaders are being challenged with the daunting task of making America's students college and career competitive in a global society. Leadership resilience is the linchpin of 21st century leadership survival and success. Allison-Napolitano's book is an insightful guide to resilience and is a *must*-read for today's leaders and aspiring leaders."

—Anita Johnson, Executive Director
National Center for Education Research and Technology (NCERT)

"I loved this book! The need for resiliency is there for anyone in a leadership position, and this book provides the reader with tips and techniques on how to maintain that resiliency."

—Dr. Robert A. Frick, Retired Superintendent
Lancaster, PA

"While reading the section on renewal, I was reminded of how important it is to change routines and relish in the beauty of what is around me on a daily basis. I got up from the computer and went on a quick walk in my desert neighborhood. The bonus was seeing a hot air balloon floating overhead! I would have missed it! The balloon reminded me to take a bird's-eye perspective on what might seem like vast problems and challenges. Kudos to this author!"

—Dr. Roseanne Lopez
Executive Director of Elementary Education

"As a school administrator how do you stay positive and continually look for ways to improve your school in the face of mounting challenges? After reading this book you will be able to stay positive and take your school to new heights."

—Jim Anderson, Principal
Andersen Jr. High School
Chandler, AZ

"Drawing on a wealth of relevant research literature, Dr. Allison-Napolitano provides practical strategies and tools for assessing and building resilience. Supported by case studies that will resonate with educational leaders, she presents a model of resilience as a discipline to be practiced. I highly recommend her book to support both novice and veteran leaders and their teams looking to continually improve individual and organizational capacity to 'bounce forward.'"

—Dr. Pamela Comfort, Associate Superintendent
Contra Costa County Office of Education
Pleasant Hill, CA

Bounce
Forward

Always for Len Mike and Olé, my two "Wilsons"
(see Chapter 3 for an explanation)

In memory of my father-in-law, Dr. Leonard M. Napolitano Sr.,
Dean of the University of New Mexico Medical School
1972 to 1994, a beloved and resilient leader.

Bounce Forward

The Extraordinary Resilience of Leadership

Elle Allison-Napolitano

Foreword by **Michael Fullan**

CORWIN
A SAGE Company

CORWIN
A SAGE Company

FOR INFORMATION:

Corwin
A SAGE Company
2455 Teller Road
Thousand Oaks, California 91320
(800) 233-9936
www.corwin.com

SAGE Publications Ltd.
1 Oliver's Yard
55 City Road
London EC1Y 1SP
United Kingdom

SAGE Publications India Pvt. Ltd.
B 1/I 1 Mohan Cooperative Industrial Area
Mathura Road, New Delhi 110 044
India

SAGE Publications Asia-Pacific Pte. Ltd.
3 Church Street
#10-04 Samsung Hub
Singapore 049483

Executive Editor: Arnis Burvikovs
Associate Editor: Desirée A. Bartlett
Editorial Assistant: Ariel Price
Production Editor: Melanie Birdsall
Copy Editor: Terri Lee Paulsen
Typesetter: C&M Digitals (P) Ltd.
Proofreader: Laura Webb
Indexer: Molly Hall
Cover Designer: Karine Hovsepian

Printed in the United States of America

Library of Congress Cataloging-in-Publication Data

Allison-Napolitano, Elle.
Bounce forward : the extraordinary resilience of leadership / Elle Allison-Napolitano.

pages cm
Includes bibliographical references and index.

ISBN 978-1-4522-7184-2 (pbk.)

1. Educational leadership. 2. Resilience (Personality trait) I. Title.

LB2806.A5255 2014
371.2—dc23   2013040432

This book is printed on acid-free paper.

14 15 16 17 18 10 9 8 7 6 5 4 3 2 1

Contents

Foreword

Elle Allison-Napolitano knows a great deal about resilience. This is a great book because she goes deeply and comprehensively into the conceptual basis of the concept, and equally and deeply into the practical actions that will be required.

Resilience is one of the prime qualities that leaders and, in fact, all of us will need under the ambiguous and tumultuous conditions we endure these days. But thanks to Allison-Napolitano, we don't have to *endure* anything because she supplies the resources of resilience that are eminently practical and uplifting.

She provides a philosophy for how to bounce back as we bounce forward. The model is simple and powerful. It is framed by renewal, resonance, and relationships. It has six strategic domains: Stay Calm, Carry On, Accept the New Reality, Want Something More, Instigate Adaptive Action, and Reflect & Celebrate. We are also treated to a daunting listing of potential adversities facing educational leaders with such categories as systemwide seismic trauma, organizational leadership gauntlets, personal and interpersonal leadership challenges, the daily churn of leadership work, and shattering personal and professional events.

In addition to clear portrayals of real-life issues, and vivid examples of situations and responses, *Bounce Forward* contains tools—easy-to-use inventories to size up our own realities. These simple but powerful tools contain just 10 items each, but they make you think, and give perspectives and ideas with respect to how to deal with each problem area. In filling out a given inventory, I found myself immediately thinking of actual events and occasions that I personally experienced. I was already having new perspectives about these situations and insights into how I could relate and react to them differently, not to mention the additional insights provided by the author herself. There are diagnostic tools on the Resilience Inventory, the Relationship Inventory, the Resonance Inventory, and the Renewal Inventory.

Allison-Napolitano then takes us into each of the strategic areas: Staying Calm, Carry On, and so on—in each case providing examples and ideas of what the domain means and feels like, and how to deal with it. Once we have a thorough understanding of the territory and ourselves therein we move to action such as a great chapter, "Organizational Resilience Risks and Opportunities," in which we consider not just how to be more resilient individually but also *organizationally*. Individuals who are leaders in schools or districts will be interested in the Resilience Risk Rubric and the "How Vulnerable Is Your Organization?" rubric.

There is not much publicly known work available on the concept of resilience, yet it is the most commonly needed response in our lives. By definition, more and more of our experiences are nonlinear and punctuated with unpredictable events. The author does not have abstract "turn the other cheek" advice. She wants us to be as tough as the circumstances require. In the final analysis we need to be softer on ourselves as we are harder on dealing with problems. *Bounce Forward* is a wonderful book that is as realistic as it is inspiring. Read it and it will take you deeper into your life—past, present, and future. It will bring you tears, but ultimately it will put a fresh bounce in your step.

—Michael Fullan

Preface

I began this book for the same reasons that I begin almost everything: to help leaders and organizations do more of what makes them effective, happy, and wise, and remove whatever diminishes them and prevents them from being great in their work and lives. As a practitioner in organizational learning, I have a passion for understanding how people and systems learn and adapt in order to accomplish desirable goals. As a simple and highly practical person, however, I'm not satisfied with studying ideas. What I really love is inventing practical tools from the best ideas "out there" as well as my own research and fieldwork, and then teaching people how to use them so they can accomplish big things.

A FOCUS ON LEADERSHIP RESILIENCE

This book wraps its covers around the concept of leadership resilience, which is the experience of helping organizations bounce forward into new realities in the face of adversity and change. Therefore, except when it aids understanding, this book will not focus on ordinary resiliency but on leadership resiliency. In addition, it does not seek to cover the entire territory of leadership during times of change, but it will focus on the extra requirements of leadership resilience during disruptive change.

To accomplish this focus, I've delved into relevant information from what is known about resilience and applied it to leadership. The literature on which I have relied is not inclusive, but it is representative from several fields of study such as psychological resilience, positive psychology, transformational leadership, posttraumatic growth, emotional intelligence, organizational learning, neuroscience, behavioral economics, and adaptive change theory. Having a long tradition of using stories and observations of real people navigating the challenges and opportunities of their lives and work, I've also bolstered the ideas and tools you'll find in this book with stories from interviews I conducted with real leaders facing adversity in their real work. After all, it is only through the job-embedded stories of what happens and what leaders do in response to what happens that we see resilience in action. Stories make resilience visible.

ORIENTATION TO THIS BOOK

In the chapters that follow, I propose a model that illuminates the concept of leadership resilience, what it takes to become a resilient leader, how to respond to adversity and disruptive change with resilience, and how to create resilient organizations.

An Inside-Out Approach

Gandhi's words, "Be the change you want to see in the world," has engendered transformational leadership in individuals from all walks of life and livelihood. When it comes to leadership resilience, Gandhi's words are ironclad, for leaders are only as resilient in their work as they are personally, and resilient organizations depend on resilient leadership. For these reasons, this book begins at the personal level and then scales to the organization. All of the ideas about resilience offered to you in this book are actionable. You can begin to practice them immediately, and over time you'll become more resilient and will inspire resilience in others.

Book Organization

Part I of this book comprises two chapters.

In **Chapter 1,** I define leadership resilience, show how it is different from ordinary resilience, and reveal its transformational qualities and nature. We'll also look at the types of adversities that strike educational leaders, and that beg for a resilient response.

In **Chapter 2,** I introduce the Leadership Resilience Model, which is composed of three parts:

1. Enabling capacities of leadership resilience, which make leadership resilience a possibility: Relationships, Resonance, and Renewal;

2. A nondirectional cycle showing six ideas that put Leadership Resilience in Action: Stay Calm, Carry On, Accept the New Reality, Want Something More, Instigate Adaptive Action, and Reflect & Celebrate; and

3. An outer circle representing the ecosystem of the organization the leader works within.

Part II comprises three chapters, each of which focuses on one of the three leadership resilience-enabling capacities. The enabling capacities make leadership resilience possible. Each chapter offers you the opportunity to complete an inventory that allows you to reflect on your current levels with regard to each enabling capacity and provide a springboard for conversation. Each chapter also contains approaches for bringing the resilience-enabling capacities to life, in complex organizational contexts.

Chapter 3 delves into the enabling capacity of Relationships—those personal and professional networks that provide support during times of adversity.

Chapter 4 illuminates the enabling capacity of Resonance—the ability of a leader to ignite the organization with emotions that help them bounce forward and take action in the aftermath of change.

Chapter 5 focuses on the importance of the enabling capacity of Renewal, which is the source of energy for sustaining leadership resilience.

Part III takes us to the second part of the Leadership Resilience Model, which focuses on Leadership Resilience in Action and is comprised of six chapters. Like the chapters before them, they offer specific strategies and tools for becoming more personally resilient and for developing as a highly resilient leader with an increasing capacity for turning sows' ears into silk purses. This section offers six primary actions:

Chapter 6. Stay Calm
Chapter 7. Carry On
Chapter 8. Accept the New Reality
Chapter 9. Want Something More
Chapter 10. Instigate Adaptive Action
Chapter 11. Reflect & Celebrate

Part IV scales resilience to organizations and presents an organizational Resilience Risk Rubric that leaders use to introduce helpful disruption and proactively deal with vulnerabilities that undermine the system.

Special Features and Suggestions

Although you certainly may read this book on your own and hopefully gain much from it, resilience is a quality acquired best from taking risks that test your mettle on the job and sharing experiences with others who are doing the same. For that reason, I wrote this book with the idea that readers would band together to read it in their leadership teams or with their mentors and coaches and colleagues. To empower you toward this end, chapters contain **"Activities and Questions for Study Groups and Teams,"** which provoke ideas about leadership resilience. You can use these activities and questions to get your own resilience juices flowing or to coach another person or team to do the same.

Here are the other special features you'll find in this book:

1. Stories, reflections, and ideas from effective leaders who love their work, achieve results, and make a difference.

2. Inventories you can take in the book or online.

3. Strategies, tools, and helpful sidebars.

4. A rubric to use with your teams and colleagues to evaluate your organization for vulnerabilities in resilience.

5. An appendix with a short list of some of my favorite movies, music, literature, and poems that for me conjure up ideas of leadership resilience. I'm sure you have your own great list too. I'd love to know what inspires you. I'm putting these ideas on the blog I have at www.WisdomOut.com.

FOLLOW-UP

The reason this book is filled with rich stories of tribulations and triumph is because we all have them. Thankfully, the good leaders whose stories and ideas appear in this book were willing to share them with me, allowing me to share them with you. Stories really are the only way we see resilience. In this spirit, I invite you to continue your journey toward leadership resilience by participating in additional professional development opportunities:

1. First, if you have a resilience story you want to share, or if you try out some of the ideas in this book and you want to tell me how it went, either e-mail me at elle@wisdomout.com or call me at 925-786-0987. I really do love learning your stories and learning from you.

2. Visit www.WisdomOut.com and sign up for the newsletter in which we provide registration links to our complimentary webinars, many of which focus on the ideas in this book.

3. Come to www.WisdomOut.com to purchase the packaged series of webinars that correspond to this book, and use them at your convenience with your leadership team or your leadership resilience study group.

4. Contact me for keynotes, workshops, and boot camps for aspiring, novice, and veteran leaders on the topic of leadership resilience. These workshops are especially successful when leadership coaches and mentors attend with their coachees and mentees.

5. Contract with me to work directly with your leadership team or work team as you launch or deepen your organizational initiatives and where being resilient will make all the difference in the world to achieving your outcomes without losing your mind or your sense of humor.

Acknowledgments

First, I need to acknowledge just how much it means to me to have Michael Fullan write the foreword to this book. Allow me to explain. Many years ago, as a novice administrator in the early 1990s, it was Michael Fullan who helped me figure out what it meant to be a school leader. Back then, Dr. Fullan did not know me personally, but whenever I was given the chance to attend state and national education conferences, I consistently showed up early and stayed late for every one of his sessions. At these conferences I ran into Dr. Fullan often in passing and would engage him in conversation when I could. Not believing that someone as awesome as he was would remember me, I would introduce myself, over and over again. Frankly, had Dr. Fullan taken out a restraining order against me at that time, he likely would be justified: Everywhere he spoke, there I would be, in the front row, urgently taking notes, nodding earnestly, and shooting him goofy smiles.

Then, in the late 1990s when I had the position of supervisor of school improvement at the Mississippi Bend Area Education Agency, and had the tremendous opportunity to develop professional development for school leaders around the earliest "model technology schools," I met Gerry Smith, who back then was principal of River Oaks Elementary School, located in Ontario, Canada. At that time, Michael and Gerry were co-collaborators on a number of leadership projects. Working with both of them, I, along with colleagues Bette Frazier and Len Dose, and with the blessing of our boss, Dick Hanzelka, led an academy for Iowa educational leaders that not only helped them embrace and apply new instructional technologies, but also helped them manage the stress of change around the organizational transformation required to adopt new tools. Needless to say, the collaboration with Michael Fullan, Gerry Smith, and the good folks at the Mississippi Bend AEA remains a pinnacle of my professional life.

And so, with this background, perhaps you understand that after more than 20 years of learning from Dr. Fullan, the fact that he has written the foreword to this book is the greatest honor I can imagine.

I also wish to extend a special word of gratitude to Anita Johnson, executive director of NCERT (National Center for Education Research and Technology), who is an extraordinary friend to senior educational leaders. Not only did Anita arrange for me to hold focus groups on the topic of resilience at NCERT gatherings, but no one I know has the compassion that Anita has for school leaders. As a former school leader, and now in her role as executive director of NCERT and as a consultant for superintendent search committees, Anita knows firsthand what it means to be a strong, authentic, and resilient leader. Her keen insights about how networks aid in resilience is reflected throughout this book.

Significantly, this book is filled with wisdom from some of the most resilient educational leaders I know, who in 2012 and 2013 either participated in NCERT focus groups, met with me in one-on-one interviews, or both. I thank them all, with all of my heart:

Pamela Auburn	Jody Leinenwever
John Aycock	Sister Marianella
Mark Bielang	Dale Marsden
Marilyn Birnbaum	Rick Miller
Mike Borgaard	Sue Page
Dan Boyd	Randy Poe
Doreen Corrente	Bettye Ray
Maggie Cuellar	Ron Richards
Bob Dubick	Dave Sholes
Carmella Franco	Rob Slaby
Rob Haley	Lloyd Snow
Lisa Harris	Cindy Weber
Janine Hoke	Patty Wool
Anita Johnson	

My gratitude also to all the professionals at Corwin who had a hand in making this book a reality, beginning with Arnis Burvikovs who first asked me to write about the unique nature of leadership resilience. Thanks also go to Desirée Bartlett, Ariel Price, Melanie Birdsall, Terri Lee Paulsen, and Karine Hovsepian.

I also wish to thank Margaret Rode from Websites for Good, who designed and has maintained the Wisdom Out website since 2006; Becky Wagley, my graphic artist; and Claire Therese LaPlante, who worked as my personal editorial assistant for this book.

Books like this one do not become a reality without the good and true support of people who support the author. For me, many good friends and family members inspire and encourage me, mostly by the way they live their lives: Nancy Ovis, Barbara Jennings, Cindy Pence, Bette Frazier,

Patsy Bovarie, Rob and Kathy Bocchino, Mary Ann Weems, Thelma Domenici, and Janet Napolitano. This esteemed group also includes my funny and loving sisters who were the first people to show me what it means to be resilient: Mary Hogan Nicks, Joanne Hogan, Dr. Mo Hogan, Beth Hogan-Chan, and Carrie Hogan, as well as their spouses Bill LaPlante, Louis Chan, and Sarah Schmidt. I also thank my nieces, nephews, and step-children, whose very existence reminds me that resilience is the only choice I have in my own life if I am to set a good example for them: Claire LaPlante, Caroline LaPlante, Adam Nicks, Lulu Nicks, Christopher Chan, Hayden Chan, Norah Hogan-Schmidt, Carrie Napolitano, and David Napolitano.

I also wish to thank Chuck and Eunjoo Lee, owners of Pasqual's French Bakery, located in my little town of Danville, California, where I was sustained by delicious waffles, eggs, oatmeal, and pastries and sat for hours working on this book. Chuck and Eunjoo always made me feel welcome and kept my coffee cup filled.

For my dog, Olé, who turned 16 years old as I wrote this book. Talk about resilience. Finally, yet really, always first, I thank my husband, Len Mike Napolitano, who is the best man I know.

PUBLISHER'S ACKNOWLEDGMENTS

Corwin gratefully acknowledges the contributions of the following reviewers:

Jim Anderson, Principal
Anderson Junior High School
Chandler, Arizona

Robert A. Frick, Superintendent (Retired)
Lampeter-Strasberg School District
Lancaster, Pennsylvania

Nicole Kemp, Principal
North Callaway R1 School District
Williamsburg, Missouri

Roseanne Lopez, Executive Director of Elementary Education
Amphitheater Unified School District
Tucson, Arizona

About the Author

Elle Allison-Napolitano, founder of Wisdom Out, specializes in leadership development and organizational learning. Dr. Allison-Napolitano works with leaders, aspiring leaders, senior leadership teams, school teams, and leadership coaches to teach them the strategies, practices, and tools they need to sustain their energy and resilience as they focus on the most important work of their organizations.

Elle has been a teacher, principal, supervisor of school improvement, assistant superintendent, educational consultant, and leadership coach. She earned her PhD in organizational learning from the University of New Mexico. She is a graduate of the National Staff Development Council's Academy and is a member of the National Speakers Association. She is author of several books and articles on leadership renewal and resilience, and on leadership coaching, including her book, *Flywheel: Transformational Leadership Coaching for Sustainable Change,* also from Corwin.

Elle lives in the San Francisco Bay area with her husband, Len, and their 16-year-old Vizsla dog named Olé. Contact Elle at elle@wisdomout.com for customized workshops, leadership academies, boot camps, and keynotes. To register for the Wisdom Out newsletter and complimentary webinars, please visit www.WisdomOut.com.

Introduction

A few Aprils ago, while I was in New Orleans to speak at a conference and hold a book signing, my house in Albuquerque, where I was living at the time, was burgled. The call from my neighbor in New Mexico arrived when I was sitting at an outdoor restaurant in the French Quarter, feeling on top of the world and pleasantly buzzed from the beer I gulped with my shrimp po' boy while listening to jazz. I had just come from watching something called "the Pirates Parade," a bawdy fundraiser for the wife and children of a fallen New Orleans police officer—a startling mixture of tragic circumstances, gallows humor, activism, and in true New Orleans style, skimpy costumes.

Prior to watching the parade, I had delivered a fun and engaging workshop at the conference for educational leaders, and I don't mind saying that I was feeling *AWESOME*. As a result, the call from my neighbor, from over 1,000 miles away, seemed preposterous. I remember thinking, "Ha-ha, my house was burgled? That's a good one! What's the punch line?"

LIFE IS HARD

And yet it was true. While I was living it up in New Orleans, my house in Albuquerque had been burgled. But here I was in the city where in 2005 Hurricane Katrina stole entire homes. Walking around, you still see evidence of the devastation—a condemned house here, a gouged-out section of land there. In New Orleans, it was unseemly to feel sorry for myself; my house might have been burgled, but I still had my home. Tempted as I was to catch the next flight back to New Mexico, I stayed put and finished my dinner. After all, I still had a commitment to speak at another conference session the next morning, and so really, there was nothing for me to do. And so, with good neighbors and friends to secure my house for the night, I decided to stay focused and carry on in New Orleans.

When I returned to New Mexico, I was unprepared for the condition of my home. It was thoroughly tossed. Every drawer, cabinet, closet, nook, and

1

cranny was ransacked. Most everything of value, along with personal and sentimental items that only mattered to me, had vanished.

For weeks after the burglary, I would reach for a common item only to find empty air and space. Five days in a row, I went for the blender to make my post-run banana protein shake, only to rediscover that it too was gone. Each time, with fresh disbelief, I stared at the void my humble blender once occupied. Then, still eyeing its former place on the countertop, I would reluctantly put away the ingredients for my shake and eat the banana whole. I missed the blender, but I was outraged to discover that the burglars actually used my own luggage to relieve me of some of my stuff. Somehow, this particular detail bugs me more than anything else. As a frequent business traveler, I had quality luggage—the kind that holds up for 20, even 30 years. I had already had mine for 10, which made the replacement price far higher than what my insurance company would reimburse me. It will take another 10 years to build my luggage assets back up to pre-burglary levels.

The Gifts of Loss

As a researcher, writer, and speaker on wisdom, resilience, and leadership, I really do try hard to learn from the gracious people from around the globe who tell me their stories and allow me to share them with others. One of the most helpful lessons has been to realize that wisdom and resilience are not synonymous with perfection. Even wise and resilient people get ticked off. But they usually don't stay upset for long. Instead of raging against the fates, they say things like, "Well isn't that interesting?" or, "Well if that don't beat all." They also have a way of seeing the gifts hidden in loss. Because they take action early after suffering a blow, windows and doors fly open before them and new opportunities appear. These hardy individuals do not linger in nostalgia for what used to be. In fact, by most accounts, they truly believe they are better off after a loss than they were before, if for no other reason than for the growth it provokes for them.

Even With Your Ducks in a Row

As I walked around my disheveled home, reminding myself "it's only stuff," and taking inventory of the missing items, there in the guest bathroom medicine cabinet I discovered another lesson in resilience, one that is enormously poignant for leaders of complex organizations. When I opened the mirrored door, I found that the little duck-shaped soaps I had placed inside a month before were still there, all in a row (see photo on page 5). And so the truth is revealed: It is not technically true that having your ducks in a row will stave off loss, disappointment, and sorrow. Rather than be floored by this astonishing realization, I find it quite freeing. Perfection is not a prerequisite for life, and there is much that is out of our circle of control. In fact, since stuff happens to us whether we have our ducks in a row or not, our energy is far better placed in transforming inevitable loss into opportunity. How to do this is the subject of this book, and more specifically, how to do it as a *leader,* when everyone is watching you, and either depending on you or daring you to confidently and elegantly take the first step.

LEARNING RESILIENCE

According to the American Psychological Association (APA), "Resilience is not a trait that people either have or do not have. It involves behaviors, thoughts and actions that can be learned and developed by anyone" (APA, 2002). Given the fact that overall the adversities that befall educational leaders are neither unusual nor uncommon, this is good news indeed and enormously hopeful; whatever your current capacity for resilience, you can and will become even more resilient. The truth is, life's daily trials and tribulations provide us all with rich, and highly differentiated resilience curricula, all within the hallowed halls of what many veteran leaders fondly refer to as The College of Hard Knocks. Therefore, the strategies you'll find throughout this book are best learned and practiced against the nitty-gritty backdrop of your real work. In addition to working the resilience strategies within real work contexts, you can accelerate your learning through working with a leadership coach—perhaps someone you can tap right there in your workplace—who will engage you in deep and powerful conversations that lead to insight and action.

FIVE GOOD REASONS FOR INCREASING YOUR LEADERSHIP RESILIENCE

1. Because even with your ducks in a row, stuff happens. Rather than rail against adversity, better to learn resilience.

2. Because you can. Resilience is not something you either have or do not have; you can learn to become more resilient.

3. Because resilient leaders achieve more goals.

4. Because resilient leaders manage the stress of change better than leaders who are not resilient.

5. Because the same characteristics of leadership resilience also make your life more joyful.

If there is anything daunting about growing in leadership resilience, it's that you can't just read about it or hear about it and expect to become more resilient, any more than you can watch the cooking channel on TV and then go into the kitchen expecting to find the same meal waiting for you at the table. Becoming more resilient comes down to your determination to change existing habits and learn new ways of being and leading in the face of adversity. Resilience may be hard won, but leaders who choose to build their personal resilience, and create resilient organizations, will understand the truth of what Friedrich Nietzsche meant when he said, "That which does not kill us makes us stronger."

SUSTAINING YOUR PRACTICE OF LEADERSHIP RESILIENCE

As with any worthwhile practice, the road to excellence begins with commitment. One highly effective strategy for keeping the commitments you make to yourself to put the ideas in this book into action is to tell at least one person about it and ask for his or her support and feedback. Here are a few additional ideas for sustaining your leadership practice of becoming more resilient:

1. Make it part of your leadership development goals. Whether you are a teacher leader or an educational administrator, you most likely have a success plan that outlines your learning goals each year. Tell the person you report to that you would like to make leadership resiliency a focus of your goals. Better yet, ask them to read this book with you and meet to talk about it.

2. Secure the services of a leadership coach or mentor and invite them to read the book with you and discuss the ideas within as part of your leadership work.

3. Keep a journal where you can reflect on the adversities you face in your leadership work and on how you responded and what you learned.

Once you make a commitment to yourself to mindfully focus on leadership resilience, take time to read this book and apply what you learn in your life. As you place your attention on the capacities and actions that make leadership resilience possible, you will cultivate more of it. Don't despair during those times when you feel less resilient. In fact, the experience of being non-resilient is actually good for you to remember, as you will better recognize what it means to bounce forward. When you forget to take guidance from what you know works, simply come back to it. As a practice, coming back to leadership resilience is always possible and always available.

BE A GOOD SOUL

At some point, even though you are not perfect in your own practice of leadership resilience, be willing to coach and mentor a new leader in their practice of bouncing forward. In these roles, you will simultaneously deepen and strengthen your leadership resilience while providing enormous comfort and support to new or aspiring leaders who no doubt face myriad adversities of their own.

Ducks in a Row

Photo Credit: Elle Allison-Napolitano 2009. No further reproduction or distribution is permitted without written permission from Elle Allison-Napolitano.

Part I

The Exceptional Nature of Leadership Resilience

1   Bounce Forward

Mike S. is the former superintendent of a large school district on the East Coast. He has been retired now for many years, but he is still widely regarded by the citizens of the city, as well as the wider educational community, as the individual who led this school district out of darkness. Over a decade ago, when Mike first stepped in, the district was plagued by low expectations for students and low student performance, especially for African Americans and students from families of meager means. By the time he retired, eight years later, the district and its students were flourishing. The percentage of students who were learning at high levels and earning awards and career opportunities and scholarships to further their education had reached unprecedented levels. Faculty, staff, and community confidence and morale had increased correspondingly, producing a "can do" climate that engendered innovation and collaboration.

During the early days of the district's transformation under Mike's leadership, Laura, one of the district principals, told me about a specific event when she first recognized Mike's remarkable leadership resilience. Laura told me that Mike made a presentation to a deeply divided school board, recommending an increase of personnel and other resources to provide rapid remediation for students needing extra learning time and instruction—many of whom attended Laura's school. Laura said, "Not only was the school board divided and giving Mike the third degree, but they had rallied community groups to show up and give him a hard time too." According to Laura, whose high-need campus was a lightning rod for the conversation, while she and other district administrators could not believe the voraciousness with which the board and community attacked Mike and his recommendation, Mike himself was steady, calm, and unwavering in his arguments and recommendation. He never reacted to the rude comments and personal attacks, even as the meeting went on late into the night.

But what Laura remembers most is that the next morning, when she and the rest of the faculty arrived early at their campus to debrief the previous evening's board meeting, there was Mike, greeting them with a smile, an enormous box of donuts, and a jug of coffee. The effect of Mike's resilience on Laura and on her faculty was powerful and set the tone for a high level of resilience throughout the organization. Laura said, "Everything about Mike showing up in the morning to help us debrief the board meeting gave us strength and forbearance. The donuts and coffee reminded us that life goes on, and contentious board meetings would not derail us. The refreshments added a celebratory tone to the meeting, which was a complete switch from the heavy 'post-mortem' tone we might have expected. The fact that Mike was there at all, and not hiding out in his office or sleeping in for that matter, after such a late night, set the expectation that not only will we withstand resistance, but through collaboration and simply making it OK to talk about it, we were capable of more than we first imagined."

THE OUTCOMES OF LEADERSHIP RESILIENCE

Instinctively, most leaders will say that resilience helps them adopt a positive perspective in the face of adversity. But the benefits of leadership resilience produce much more than a positive and optimistic disposition; it is also essential to reaching goals and to achieving organizational outcomes. Before reading the list in the Benefits of Leadership Resilience box, jot your own bulleted list of the benefits of leadership resilience to you and your organization. How does your list compare with the ideas presented?

BENEFITS OF LEADERSHIP RESILIENCE

1. Resilience is a proactive way to respond to disruptive change, challenges, and adversity.

2. Resilience establishes a culture of achievement. It helps you sustain your focus on school and district outcomes.

3. Resilient leaders get things done. When they say they are going to do something they stick with it, and they follow through and this builds their reputations as trustworthy leaders.

4. Resilient leaders are valued employees for their record of accomplishment, and may receive opportunities and promotions over their less resilient but otherwise qualified peers.

5. Resilience helps you manage the stress that naturally occurs around change initiatives.

6. Your resilience sets a cultural example for the next generation of leaders. How you respond to adversity creates a template for how the organization and community responds to adversity.

7. Persistence in problem solving often leads to breakthrough thinking, creativity, ingenuity, and innovation.

8. Resilience makes leadership visible. Controversy and challenges are defining moments for leaders—people watch how you respond during times of adversity, and they form enduring impressions to define you from that point forward.

Leaders like Mike S. (from the story presented above) appear to have a knack for responding to adversity and unexpected change with maturity, equanimity, grace, courage, and pluck. But highly resilient leaders like Mike could not repeatedly face such daunting scenarios and reap the benefits of leadership resilience without experiencing what it feels like to do so. Thankfully, whether or not we become highly resilient leaders, we all possess ordinary resilience, which helps us get our foot into the door. Ordinary resilience helps leaders stay in the game long enough to grow the deeper levels of resilience required by the demands of leadership.

ORDINARY RESILIENCE

Before we leap into our exploration of leadership resilience, I want to briefly set the stage by first laying out what it means to have ordinary resilience; what it means to *bounce back* in the aftermath of challenges and disruptive change.

The American Psychological Association (APA) captures the essence of resilience in this definition: "Resilience is the process of adapting well in the face of adversity, trauma, tragedy, threats, or even significant sources of stress—such as family and relationship problems, serious health problems, or workplace and financial stressors. It means 'bouncing back' from difficult experiences" (APA, 2002). Like the APA, many contemporary researchers of resilience highlight the role of adaptation in resilience and explore what it means to bounce back. A highly regarded researcher on bereavement and resilience, George Bonanno (2009) elaborates on the process of adapting well by describing resilient people as those who bounce back and continue forward in life with a sense of core purpose and meaning. Expanding the scope of resilience beyond individuals, researchers Zolli and Healy (2012) define resilience as "the capacity of a system, enterprise, or a person to maintain its core purpose and integrity in the face of dramatically changed circumstances" (p. 126). Writing about resilience in young people, Clay, Knibbs, and Joseph (2009) say resilience is "the ability to continue to function normally in spite of adversity" (p. 413), and Scales, Benson, Leffert, and Blyth (2000) describe it as the ability to overcome negative events and quickly return to pretrauma levels of functioning.

Given the widely accepted definition of resilience as the ability to bounce back and carry on with life, what might seem amazing is the fact that most people *are* resilient even in the face of significant loss and challenge.

Beautifully Ordinary

In their book about why people, organizations, systems, and entire communities bounce back in the aftermath of hardship, Andrew Zolli and Ann Marie Healey (2012) relate early investigations in the field of psychological resilience and explain why we are often surprised to learn that most of us are, in fact, quite resilient. Zolli and Healy tell us that initially, resilience research focused on children who were survivors of the Nazi concentration camps or offspring of schizophrenic parents. Many of these children went on to live good and productive lives, in spite of their harsh experiences. Dominated by Freud's theory that grief is a lengthy and treacherous process, however, the social psychologists that studied these children believed they were witnessing "superkids" who were blessed with an unusual ability to cope. But one researcher, named Ann Masten, pointed out that while it certainly was amazing that these children thrived in the face of such hardship, it was not *unusual* that they did so. The reason, Masten said, is the presence of "basic human adaptational systems" (Zolli & Healy, 2012, p. 122) that predispose all of us for bouncing back.

Resilience in Common

Again, according to the APA (2002), "Research has shown that resilience is ordinary, not extraordinary. People commonly demonstrate resilience. One example is the response of many Americans to the September 11, 2001, terrorist attacks and individuals' efforts to rebuild their lives." Martin Seligman, who is often called the father of positive psychology and who leads a resiliency training program for the United States military, says that how people respond to adversity is normally distributed, with the majority of people falling in the middle (2011b). In the middle are the resilient people—those who experienced a hardship but who bounced back physically and psychologically to where they were before the trauma. According to Seligman, on the lower end of the curve are the people who develop posttraumatic stress disorder (PTSD), and at the opposite end are those individuals who eventually experience posttraumatic growth.

George Bonanno's longitudinal studies on resilience after tragedies, such as natural disasters, the SARS epidemic, or even personal losses, reveal similar findings: Only about one-third of the population experiences PTSD while the rest either bounce back or show little effect to begin with. Posttraumatic growth experts Calhoun and Tedeschi (1995) are even more optimistic. They tell us that anywhere between 30% and up to 90% of the population actually experience growth eventually, as a result of facing serious trauma.

Interestingly, Zolli and Healy say that the fact that the percentage of people who display resilience is greater than the percentage of people who display signs of PTSD or other maladaptive responses to challenges suggests that this natural design "ensures that there is always at least a sizable minority or even a majority, to take care of those deeply affected by trauma" (2012, p. 127).

What It Means to Be Resilient

Bouncing back is seen in what individuals do in the aftermath of disruptive change, particularly in the capacity they have to navigate toward resources that restore them after a setback (Zautra, Hall, & Murray, 2010). Resources might be physical, such as taking on a second job to mitigate a financial blow or installing rails in the bathroom to aid mobility after an illness. They could be social, such as establishing a new relationship or alliance with someone who can provide support, or they could be psychological, such as seeking out a therapist or learning how to reframe negative thoughts.

Being resilient does not mean that people do not feel distress, sadness, or anger. In fact, even people who are ultimately strengthened by adversity may first traverse through a period of time looking decidedly non-resilient, perhaps even feeling depressed or anxious or even turning to drugs and alcohol. But in general, we see resiliency in the capacity of people to navigate toward resources that allow them to absorb relatively high levels of disruptive change while exhibiting minimal unproductive behaviors that impede their ability to function.

The idea that resiliency is seen in people who experience setbacks but who cope and adjust so that they can return to their previous state of normal functioning lends credence to the visual image of people "bouncing back." The ability to bounce back from life's curve balls is what helps us make it through another day.

Factors That Mediate Resilience

The factors that promote resilience are many and varied, providing countless pathways for its development. A few prominent factors that appear in the literature include personality traits such as optimism and confidence (Bonanno, 2009; Bonanno, Galea, Bucciareli, & Vlahov, 2007; Seligman, 2011a), perceptions of control, feeling empowered to act, perceptions of the harm caused as a result of adversity and the extent to which it was intentional and permanent

(Calhoun & Tedeschi, 2006), having self-agency to make plans and leverage resources in one's direction and delay immediate reward in order to achieve future goals (APA, 2002; Block & Block, 1980), the presence of strong social networks, mindfulness meditation and cognitive reframing, the ability to regulate emotions, thinking and believing that one has a meaningful purpose in life, that one can influence their surroundings, and that negative experiences can indeed lead to learning and growth (Kobasa, 1979).

According to Zolli and Healy (2012), personal resilience is a habit. They say, "Whether cultivated through wise mentors, vigorous exercise, access to green space, or a particularly rich relationship with faith, the habits of personal resilience are habits of mind—making them habits we can cultivate and change when armed with the right resources" (p. 130).

LEADERSHIP RESILIENCE

To my extreme mortification I grow wiser every day.

—Lady Mary Wortley Montagu

Fortified with this foundational understanding that resilience is quite ordinary—that most of us are blessed with basic human systems of adaptation that allow us to soldier on in spite of incredible adversity—then what makes leadership resilience different? Why do leaders need to cultivate a type of resilience that is anything more or anything different from ordinary resilience?

The simple answers to these questions are found in the extraordinary demands of leadership within complex, ambiguous, and constantly changing systems. Bottom line: If ordinary resilience is *bouncing back* and resuming the path one has been on, then leadership resilience is *bouncing forward* and leading not just oneself, but others, into new and ambiguous realities. Following the famous words of Yogi Berra who reportedly advised, "When you reach a fork in the road, take it," leadership resilience is seen as your ability to make the most of every fork in the road and inspire others to walk with you with confidence.

Faster and Stronger

Given that most people are in fact resilient, it should come as no surprise that most leaders are resilient too. What may be interesting to learn, however, is that some people, including successful leaders, are more resilient than others. In his book *The Resiliency Advantage: Master Change, Thrive Under Pressure, and Bounce Back From Setbacks* (2005), the late Al Siebert compares people who are highly resilient to those who linger or remain in less resilient states, where they feel victimized by the circumstances of life. Siebert writes, "Highly resilient people are flexible, adapt to new circumstances quickly, and thrive in constant change. Most important, they expect to bounce back and feel confident that they will. They have a knack for creating good luck out of circumstances that many others see as bad luck" (p. 2).

Based on Siebert's observations, my research illuminates similar qualities of highly resilient individuals. Since 2009, I've been looking at data from leaders who complete an inventory that I use in my leadership coaching and consulting practice. The inventory provides a snapshot of an individual's status with regard to certain leadership choices necessary to facilitate sustainable change—perhaps the most challenging demand of leadership. Leadership resilience is one of the seven choices evaluated in this inventory. (The other choices are renewal, resonance, relationships, reality, recognition, and reciprocity. You can take the entire online version at www.WisdomOut.com, or you can take the individual assessments provided in this book.) In addition to exploring levels of the seven characteristics, the inventory also asks participants to rate themselves on a scale of 1 to 10 for happiness and meaningful work.

What I have found is that leaders who rate themselves high on happiness and engagement in meaningful work also score in the "amazingly resilient" category of resilience 70% more often than participants who rate themselves low on happiness and engagement in meaningful work. Effective and happy leaders are so darn resilient, in fact, that they might even appear to others to be immune to fearsome forces of nature. Extraordinarily resilient people do seem to operate with a certain amount of indifference to life's travails (Calhoun & Tedeschi, 2006). These findings, combined with the stories of leadership resilience that I gather from my fieldwork, confirm what others are saying about the resilience of successful leaders: They respond faster, stronger, wiser, and with a greater amount of pluck and good cheer than leaders who are not as successful.

Resilience Inventory

Bearing in mind that resilience can be learned, the following inventory will provide you with a current snapshot of your *personal* resilience (for a computerized administration of this inventory, log on to www.WisdomOut.com, and click on "Assessments"). You can take this inventory several times per year—perhaps once every quarter—as a way to focus on different facets of resilience. (Note: If you are reading this book as a leadership team, replace "I" with "We.")

Instructions: Respond to each of the statements in Exercise 1.1 quickly, providing your first impulse as the answer. If you are responding as a team, look at the average response or look at the amount of responses for each number in the range. A response of 10 is the strongest possible agreement, and 1 is the strongest possible disagreement. There are no correct answers. However, the inventory will be most useful to you if you provide the most authentic response, and that is likely to be the first response that comes to mind.

Exercise 1.1 The Personal Resilience Inventory

Statement	Strongly Disagree								Strongly Agree	
1. Almost every week, I encounter a situation that is past my breaking point. I don't know if I can bounce back from it.	1	2	3	4	5	6	7	8	9	10
2. When I encounter failure, the causes are almost always factors beyond my control.	1	2	3	4	5	6	7	8	9	10
3. When I suffer professional disappointments, I doubt I can ever make it up to my boss, team, or my organization.	1	2	3	4	5	6	7	8	9	10
4. The last time I suffered a personal loss such as the loss of a friend, partner, or family member, I felt life could never be as good as it once was.	1	2	3	4	5	6	7	8	9	10
5. If I ask for help from colleagues, they will know that I am incapable of doing adequate work on my own.	1	2	3	4	5	6	7	8	9	10
6. When I encounter silence in relationships, it usually means that the other person is disappointed or angry with me.	1	2	3	4	5	6	7	8	9	10
7. When I think of tragic events in the news or in history, most of them were just unavoidable.	1	2	3	4	5	6	7	8	9	10
8. The significant changes that have happened in my life were usually caused by forces outside my control.	1	2	3	4	5	6	7	8	9	10
9. In the past year, I have attempted to make a major personal change, but outside influences prevented me from following through on it.	1	2	3	4	5	6	7	8	9	10
10. In the past year, I have thought about or attempted to make an important professional change, but I could not get the support from organizations and those "in charge" to make it work.	1	2	3	4	5	6	7	8	9	10

Total score: _____

Reflection on Your Score: With a pen or highlighter, flag the sentences below that "speak to you" for whatever reason. Some sentences may seem "right on target." Others might seem off the mark. Don't dismiss the "off the mark" sentences immediately. Instead, reflect alone or with a trusted person or leadership coach about what they might mean.

Interpreting Your Score

Where do highly resilient leaders tend to score on the Resilience Inventory? Leaders who take the online version of the Resilience Inventory, and who also rate themselves high on happiness and meaningful work, score most often in the range of 0–25.

If You Scored in the Range of 0–25: You are an amazingly resilient person. When you encounter disappointments, you bounce back quickly and you hit the ground running. Likely, you are confident in your ability to learn from experience and feel almost certain that you can influence the results the next time. This doesn't mean you avoid the adversities of life, but you are able to see adversity as an opportunity for growth and change. This strong confidence in your ability and healthy skepticism of the influences of the outside world will generally serve you well. However, others may sometimes see your confidence as indifference to the forces of nature and society. Therefore, you must not forget that others around you may not be as resilient as you are. Find out how you can help to mitigate the impact of adversity for those around you. Ask what they need, and provide resources and emotional support that help others who are less resilient find their way.

If You Scored in the Range of 26–50: You are a moderately resilient person, fairly confident in your abilities to withstand the slings and arrows of outrageous fortune, or at least of daily life. Your amiability and self-confidence are balanced by a healthy understanding of outside influences on your personal and professional success. In the face of disruption, however, your equinimity is not always balanced with action in response to new realities. Others may interpret this inconsistency as a sign that you do not always see the connection between events and your role in events or in your agency to respond to events. You will benefit from clarifying your analysis of situations and expressing your perceptions to those around you. For example, when you encounter a disappointment, it will be helpful if you articulate clearly where your personal responsibility begins and the impact of outside forces ends, and commit to actions within your circle of influence and control.

If You Scored in the Range of 51–75: You will benefit from an explicit focus on improving your personal resilience. Your life experiences have influenced your thought patterns in a troubling way, robbing you of confidence in your own abilities to influence your future. This can create a sense of fatalism that becomes a self-fulfilling prophesy. If you think things cannot improve, then they probably will not. If you believe that your influence on events around you is limited, then you will probably be correct. You would benefit from focusing on some very short-term (one- to four-day) objectives in which you can demonstrate your ability to influence your own life and have an impact on events around you. Rather than pursue an overwhelmingly large objective and risk disappointment, consider the pursuit of a series of small victories. The cumulative effect of them might surprise you.

If You Scored in the Range of 76–100: You have suffered serious personal and professional setbacks, and because you are convinced that these disappointments are beyond your control, you are heading toward a future of despair unless you take serious and immediate corrective action. Your support structure at home and at work may have abandoned you, as your cloud of bleak disappointment tends to scare away those who might try to offer assistance. While you may think that you are simply being open and honest about the way the world is, your views can strike others as bleak and foreboding, and therefore even people who care about you do not spend much time around you. That makes for a very lonely and disappointing life, which worsens the cycle of solitude, anger, and cynicism in which you find yourself. Fortunately, there are skills you can develop that will lead to resilience and renewal, but this will require some intense focus and concentration on a daily, even an hourly, basis. You will need to check your thought patterns for accuracy and engage in resilience exercises that will allow you to demonstrate your impact on your life and on the world around you. You deserve to have a much happier life than you have right now.

More Like Posttraumatic Growth

Resilient leaders also tend to be highly resilient individuals. These individuals sustain an aura of leadership in the face of adversity *and* they bounce forward quickly; they regain their footing and they hit the ground running. The ability to be highly resilient *and* bounce forward into new realities makes leadership resilience closer to what we see in the phenomenon known as posttraumatic growth rather than ordinary resilience. Like posttraumatic growth, which involves movement beyond pretrauma levels of adaptation (Tedeschi & Calhoun, 2004), leadership resilience has a quality of transformation about it—it is not about staying the same, it is about becoming better as a result of the hardship. This is growth that requires a transformed perspective—one that emerges only after assumptions have been challenged, broken down, and revealed. Transformation from adversity is a coveted prize.

Positive Effects of Negative Events

Coined by Tedeschi and Calhoun (1996), the term posttraumatic growth deals with the surprisingly positive effects that come from negative events. According to Tedeschi and Calhoun, the positive effects resulting from posttraumatic growth show up in five forms: (1) a sense that because of the crisis, new opportunities and possibilities have emerged; (2) how people see relationships, including a greater appreciation for people and a sense of being closer to them; (3) a greater sense of efficacy, confidence, and strength; (4) a greater appreciation for life overall, including a broader philosophy about what matters and a greater sense of fulfillment and meaning; and (5) deepened spirituality or a significant change in one's belief system.

Such is the case of Beth, a novice middle school principal who got off on the wrong foot with key members of her administrative team, resulting in their request to transfer to other schools. Beth was understandably upset about the situation and recognized the accrued gaffes she made that led to the team's disenchantment with her. She told me, "Although I can't make the two assistant principals stay and give me another chance, I can move forward from this point, learn from my mistakes, and be a better leader for the new team coming in." Beth added, "Sure, my confidence was shaken and I was even afraid I might be demoted. But I reached out to the people around me and now I know that the only way to get things accomplished as a leader is through others. The bigger lesson here is that this is exactly what we teach our students. I'm embarrassed to think that I was not the best role model for working well with others. Thank goodness I have a compassionate supervisor who wants me to succeed and will coach me through this. She even invited me to come to a panel discussion at a regional conference for novice leaders."

When we analyze Beth's story through the lens of posttraumatic growth, we can see each element at work:

A Sense of New Possibilities and Opportunities. Beth looks forward to being a better leader in the second year of her principalship. Also, Beth is astonished to find that instead of ostracizing her, her supervisor actually invited her to a conference where she can learn and grow.

Changes in Relationships With Others. The vulnerability that Beth felt when she found herself facing this leadership challenge caused her to reach out to others. Self-disclosure about the situation and how she feels about it activated a network of people, including her supervisor who could introduce new and different points of view out of which will help her make better future decisions. Beth's willingness to accept help makes her more collaborative, and in Beth's case increases her sensitivity about the importance of relationships overall and poignantly those with her leadership team.

Perceived Change in Self With Greater Efficacy and Confidence. Beth expresses feeling more confident and able to act on the lessons she learned. She feels that the way she came through this challenge makes her a better leader. She is more experienced, more self-assured, and feels confident she will face future difficulties with competence, collaboration, and compassion.

Changes in Philosophy. Although Beth will not have a second chance with her first leadership team (since two members transferred to different schools), she is deeply appreciative that she has a chance to be a different kind of leader for the new team. When it comes to making leadership decisions now, collaboration with others is now at the top of Beth's list.

Deepened Spirituality or a Significant Change in One's Belief System. Beth returned to the fundamental values that brought her to the field of education in the first place—her commitment to students and to doing what is best for them.

Resilient leaders like Beth actually appear to thrive in conditions that bring others down—they become better because of the way they work through each adversity. They value learning in all forms and are especially bolstered by hard-won lessons. These insights do not rest as dormant and interesting pieces of information; they instead become key tenets for guiding new decisions. Leaders who demonstrate this high level of resilience exemplify the saying, "When the going gets tough, the tough get going." This is the sort of leadership resilience that creates opportunity. It is more than steadiness in the face of adversity and stress—it is also the gumption to navigate toward sustaining resources that provide the grit required to actually transform the situation from one of hardship to one of opportunity.

It seems important at this point to emphasize that resilient leaders do not dodge adversity or escape the vagaries of life. Resilient leaders feel pain, become distressed, and some days they go home and cry. But they do exhibit high levels of resiliency, and they experience growth from the way they face adversity. They and others see them as having been made wiser by the challenge and the lessons learned.

THE REQUIREMENTS OF LEADERSHIP: WHAT MAKES LEADERSHIP RESILIENCE MORE CHALLENGING

When it comes to resilience, leaders bear a great responsibility. In the face of adversity, leaders must exhibit high levels of resilience and segue the resulting momentum into growth and change, not just for themselves, but for the entire organization. Management expert Tom Peters even links behaviors that are decidedly resilient to the development of trust. He says, "But as a subordinate, I trust a leader who shows up, makes the tough calls, takes the heat, sleeps well amidst the furor, and then aggressively chomps into the next task in the morning with visible vitality" (Peters, 2001). As we saw through the story of Mike S. at the start of this chapter, the resilience of the leader influences the resilience of the people they lead. Like Mike, leaders must regain their leadership footing quickly, while they simultaneously lead forward into emerging and ambiguous realities.

The Vicissitudes of Complex Organizations

During times of adversity and change, leaders face strong organizational forces that create drag and make resilience development a priority. Resistance to these antagonistic forces is futile and even counterproductive. They are inherent to complex organizations and may even serve to create a level of suffering necessary to transformational change and posttraumatic growth. The best a leader can do then is to expect them, embrace them, and understand them. Consider this list of organizational forces that make resilience a leadership priority:

- You usually have little transition time between the challenging event and your next move—even when your next move is to mindfully take a step back and gather additional information.
- Progress must continue. You are expected to manage goals upward to achieve new levels of performance. This is true even when the resources you've depended on change, or are reduced or eliminated.
- You must lead others, many of whom are resistant to change, not through control and coercion, but through influence.
- The shared purpose and vision of the organization is yoked to your resilience—a reality that requires you to develop deep understanding about what it takes to promote organizational learning and growth.
- People expect more from leaders. Leaders must adhere to higher standards and expectations. Maladaptive responses during times of adversity open you to criticism and diminish your reputation.
- Your own sense of loss and disillusionment may be very great indeed. Even so, you must manage your own emotions and help the people around you manage theirs.
- The previous reality no longer exists or has been significantly altered. Therefore, to force a return to a previous existence is unhelpful and lacks courage. It is illusionary—not visionary.
- More often than not, you must step into new or emerging realities, and therefore must leverage resources for contexts that are still undefined, unstable, and ambiguous.

- In order to take advantage of the opportunities that emerge with change, you need to be more open to learning and be more open to having your assumptions and schemas changed.

THE STRESSES OF EDUCATIONAL LEADERSHIP: NEITHER RARE NOR UNUSUAL

In the aftermath of tragic acts of violence such as what happened at Columbine, Colorado, and more recently in Newtown, Connecticut, it is tempting to say that the world has become more dangerous, more untenable, more unkind. In truth the world is neither more benevolent nor more evil than it has ever been, and the people who populate it are capable of equal amounts of extraordinary kindness and disdain. This is how it is.

Resilience experts concur; adversity is neither rare nor unusual. When I think back to my first year and a half as a novice principal, I have to agree. Here are just a few of the disruptive challenges that in many ways were the crucibles of my first principalship:

- We opened and moved to a newly constructed school with reconstituted faculty, staff, and students.
- We attempted but failed to remove letter grades from the report card in grades K through 3.
- We rewrote the curriculum to reflect a new set of content standards, and a religious group protested when we explored outcome-based education.
- The fifth-grade classes found a person who died in the woods behind our school.
- Someone broke into the school and stole the safe from the main office, including all of our petty cash.
- We had an intruder alert and were forced to lock down the school for several hours when a rampaging father and son stormed through the neighborhood after robbing a local bank, with the state police in hot pursuit.
- A teacher filed a grievance against me because she thought I visited the classes too often.

To be sure, joy over-shadowed my first principalship much more than hardship ever could, but I share these examples to emphasize the truth in the statement that disruptive change is neither unusual nor rare.

Given the subjectivity of the causes of distress in education, it is impossible to fully enumerate and describe every trauma that could befall educational leaders now or in the future. The best we can do is lay out the broad categories of such adversities and provide examples. Table 1.1 shows types and examples of adversities faced by educational leaders. As you see, some adversities are seismic to leaders both as human beings and within their leadership role. Other adversities are part and parcel of leadership—yet still could be perceived by individuals as either traumatic or passé, depending on the leader's capacity for resiliency.

Educational leaders are no different from the general population, and their resiliency has much to do with how they perceive and choose to frame the adversities they face. For any one of the educational leadership adversities presented in Table 1.1, leaders can choose to respond with resilience.

Table 1.1 Potential Adversities Facing Educational Leaders

Systemwide Seismic Trauma
• Hurricanes, tornados, and other natural disasters that destroy schools and communities
• Terrorism
• Campus intruder violence
• School violence committed by students
• The sudden and unexpected death of students or faculty/staff
• Unsafe schools: Bullying, gangs, and hate crimes
• Discrimination against subgroups of students
• Criminal charges against students or members of the faculty
Organizational Leadership Gauntlets
• Persistent gaps in student achievement and pervasive beliefs that not all students can learn
• Not reaching student achievement goals or closing achievement gaps
• Resistance to implementing the strategies of the organization
• Stakeholder resistance to change
• Anxiety in the face of implementation dips
• State and federal budget cuts
• Introduction of new laws, rules, and regulations
• Having to let go or pink-slip peers, colleagues, faculty, and staff
• Data that exposes favored illusions or challenges the current course of action

(Continued)

(Continued)

- Having to reduce resources to programs and people
- Being the bearer of information that people find upsetting
- Having your school, district, or organization placed on an improvement list by an external standard board
- Loss of resources and support for programs
- New technologies and trends that require new operating paradigms
- Being reassigned
- Losing a team member to reassignment
- Miscommunications and misunderstandings between key people and groups
- Labor grievances and strikes
- Loss of support from key stakeholders
- Unpleasant physical workplace environments
- Procedures and processes that create hoops to jump through and delay progress

Personal and Interpersonal Leadership Gauntlets

- People not working well together; difficult interpersonal relationships
- Receiving unexpected, negative feedback
- Being unprepared for a meeting, conversation, or presentation
- Learning that you acted on incorrect or incomplete information
- Showing poor judgment or making decisions that had unintended and negative impacts
- Being dressed down publicly
- Collegial isolation
- Being the target of a bully, backstabber, liar, gossiper, or someone who takes credit for your work

The Daily Churn of Leadership Work

- Overload of tasks
- Lacking skill with a new piece of technology or new approach
- Technology and equipment failures
- Unexpected interruptions and urgent requests
- Persistent interruptions
- Miscommunications and misunderstandings
- Lack of clarity in directions and expectations

- Timeline breeches

- Breeches of protocol and norms

- Unproductive meetings

- Not knowing how to manage requests

- Feeling overwhelmed, overloaded, and unproductively busy

- Lacking a skill or a key piece of information

- Misreading a situation and needing to backpedal

Shattering Personal/Professional Gauntlets

- Being fired for cause

- Having your contract non-renewed

- Facing lawsuits

- Alcohol or other addictions that come to light on the job or in the community

- Being arrested or receiving a DUI

- Being in an abusive relationship

- Being accused or found guilty of a crime

- Being accused or found guilty of violating harassment laws

- Feeling and believing that you lack moral strength as a person or as a leader

- Personal indiscretions that come to light

Clearly, not all of the challenges that hit educational leaders need to have a seismic emotional impact. Many would still agree that a leader's perception and response to stress, loss, crisis, and challenge is personal and highly subjective. What counts as a devastating blow to one school leader may be perceived by another as an expected or even interesting development. For example, in a study of the effects of stress on principals and superintendents who had to make decisions about where to cut budgets—and be the bearers of the bad news to the faculty and school community—researchers Ginsberg and Multon (2011) report that these individuals not only got less sleep and exercise, but they felt less joy for their work and felt like they were living in survival mode. On the other hand, and we may eventually see this in the subjects of Ginsberg and Multon's study, resilient leaders often eventually credit the most difficult circumstances and phases in their lives with giving them the skills and experience they need to handle the demands of the future.

MOVING ON TO CHAPTER 2:
A MODEL OF LEADERSHIP RESILIENCE

What we've established in this first chapter is that when it comes to leadership during times of adversity and unexpected change, bouncing back is not an option. Leaders must bounce forward. They must regain their footing quickly and simultaneously inspire action within new realities. Moreover, leaders must transform the hardships they face as leaders into growth and change for themselves and for the organization. Drawing on ideas from leadership, resilience, and posttraumatic growth, in the next chapter I present a model that describes a way to do this.

2 A Model of Leadership Resilience

I f ordinary resilience is the ability to bounce back to previous levels of functioning with little emotional, physical, and psychological fallout, then leadership resilience is the ability to bounce forward *into change.* The good news is that bouncing forward does not just create benefits in your leadership work. The very traits that make you a resilient leader will also enrich your life.

THE LEADERSHIP RESILIENCE MODEL

Theoretical models make visible our tacit assumptions and beliefs about how the world works. However, as we change and as the world around us changes, our assumptions and beliefs also evolve. Thus, over time, theoretical models become outmoded and in need of revision, and as George Box (Box & Draper, 1987) famously said, "All models are wrong but some are useful" (p. 424). To the extent that they are relevant and useful, theoretical models give us a way to understand universal human experiences.

The Leadership Resilience Model, depicted in Figure 2.1, has three parts:

Part 1. A tetrahedron anchored on the three corners by the enabling capacities of leadership resilience: Relationships, Resonance, and Renewal

Part 2. A nondirectional cycle inside the tetrahedron showing the six Leadership Resilience Actions: Stay Calm, Carry On, Accept the New Reality, Want Something More, Instigate Adaptive Action, and Reflect & Celebrate

Part 3. An outer circle that represents the larger ecosystem of the organization the leader works within

Taken together, the three sections of the Leadership Resilience Model describe a practice of leadership resilience. A brief explanation of each part of the model will aid you as you ponder Figure 2.1.

Figure 2.1 The Leadership Resilience Model With Three Parts

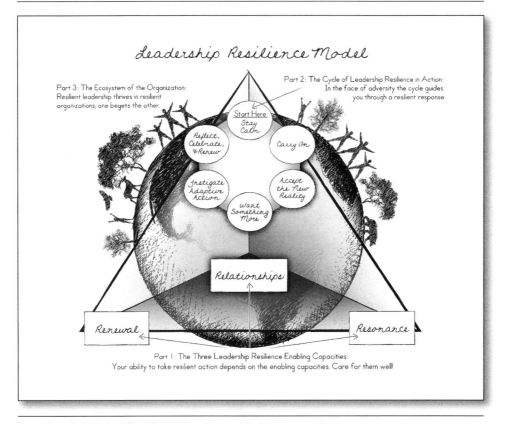

Part 1. The Leadership Resilience-Enabling Capacities: Relationships, Resonance, and Renewal

The tetrahedron at the center of the model is anchored on each corner by three leadership resilience-enabling capacities: Relationships, Resonance, and Renewal. The three leadership resilience-enabling capacities fuel resilient actions in leaders when they find themselves in the midst of disruptive change. Think of the enabling capacities as personal, sustainable, and long-term resources that empower leaders to quickly ramp up and respond with leadership resiliency when it is needed. Since Chapters 3 through 5 explore the three enabling capacities in detail, I provide only a brief summary of each here:

Relationships. In the context of leadership resilience, relationships refer to the linked networks of people and organizations that support leaders and the work of leaders. These networks mobilize resources and support to leaders at times of adversity. Leaders with strong and diverse networks find support when they need it the most (see Chapter 3 for more).

Resonance. Leaders with high levels of resonance have the ability to move people to action. Resonant leaders are adept in emotional intelligence. They regulate their emotions well, which in turn helps others do the same. In the aftermath of adversity, the effect of leadership resonance creates an environment where insightful action is possible (see Chapter 4 for more).

Renewal. Resilient leaders purposefully feed their physical, emotional, intellectual, and spiritual beings. They have identified what creates energy for themselves so they can "show up" for their lives and for the important work they do. Resilient leaders tend to gain energy from doing meaningful work and so they mindfully balance life and work so they can do the work they love, for as long as they wish (see Chapter 5 for more).

"Antifragile"

Leaders who mindfully develop and caretake the three leadership resilience-enabling capacities increase their "antifragility"—a term coined by Nicholas Taleb from the New York Polytechnic Institute in Brooklyn that seems fitting in this context. Although Taleb vehemently differentiates antifragility from resilience, leadership resilience—which is the ability to bounce forward in the face of adversity—exhibits the same form of progression as antifragility and therefore has much in common with Taleb's premise. Taleb says, "Antifragility is beyond resilience or robustness. The resilient resists shock and stays the same; the antifragile gets better" (2012, p. 3). Taleb says that fragility and antifragility are degrees on a spectrum and both can be detected "using a simple test of asymmetry: anything that has more upside than downside from random events (or certain shocks) is antifragile; the reverse is fragile" (p. 5). The enabling capacities increase the likelihood of leadership resilience. They increase the leader's ability to be wiser, stronger, and more relevant in the aftermath of disruptive change, and therefore they share similar elements to Taleb's concept of antifragility.

Part 2. Leadership Resilience in Action

And now we move to the second part of the Leadership Resilience Model. At the center of the tetrahedron is a cycle of Leadership Resilience in Action, represented by six steps or phases that describe what resilient leaders do in response to the adversities that befall them and the systems they lead. The steps are: Stay Calm, Carry On, Accept the New Reality, Want Something More, Instigate Adaptive Action, and Reflect & Celebrate.

(Chapters 6 through 11 detail the actions and provide strategies for engaging them.) The nondirectional continuous cycle implies that a leader's resilient response to adversity requires all six actions be executed in the order presented, with the option of returning to a previous action as needed. Understandably, some might perceive a cycle as rigid and over-constraining. At the same time, most agree that the actions presented in the cycle cumulatively initiate and complete a resilient response—one that is visible to anyone watching the leader as he or she faces adversity. Thus, the presentation of a simple cycle of action isolates important aspects of what in reality is a complex and intuitive response, and allows us to make a study of them.

The leadership resilience actions do more than offer a helpful framework for how to respond to challenges and adversities as a leader. They also describe how a leader becomes more resilient—for growth does not occur as a direct result of challenges, but in the struggle with the new reality in the aftermath of the challenge (Tedeschi & Calhoun, 2004).

The events that trigger the cycle of Leadership Resilience in Action usually are not the single, small annoyances that populate most days. Instead, they are events that test your assumptive world (Tedeschi & Calhoun, 2004). Resilience-triggering events are the disruptive changes and disorienting dilemmas that bring you up short, cause you to rethink, and often lead you back to the drawing board. Difficult as they are, these events also hold the most promise for transformational change (Mezirow, 2000).

When adversity strikes, Leadership Resilience in Action (Part 2 of the model) draws on the three enabling capacities of Relationships, Resonance, and Renewal (Part 1 of the model). When the enabling capacities are robust, leaders are more able to respond to adversity with agility and grace. As an additional benefit, leaders who activate the resilience actions become engaged in active problem solving, which is a strategy for coping with adversity and is related to positive long-term outcomes (Butler et al., 2005). Reflecting back to when she worked as a principal, Doreen Corrente, executive director of the Rhode Island Center for School Leadership, would seem to agree. Corrente told me, "I went through many situations where people told me something could not be done." Corrente would tell her colleagues, "This is as simple as problem solving; let's look at what is standing in our way and brainstorm ways to take it down, either in whole or in part."

A Brief Word About Crisis Response

Just to be clear, the leadership resiliency actions found at the center of the model are *not* the same thing at all as a crisis response plan. Your crisis response plan, of course, describes macro procedures and decision points in response to a crisis such as severe weather, campus intrusions, and other emergencies. In the aftermath of any one of these events, however, the

Leadership Resilience Model and the ideas in this book become useful tools for you to employ.

Part 3. The Ecosystem of the Organization

The third part of the Leadership Resilience Model is the outer circle in the image of the earth, which represents the organization: the ecosystem and culture in which the leader leads. The relationship between resilient leadership and resilient organizations is highly reciprocal. Resilient leaders create resilient organizations, and in turn, resilient organizations cultivate resilient leaders. It is here, against the scrim of complex educational organizations, that leaders have the opportunity to grow in resilience.

In its broadest terms, the organization and its prevailing culture are also the source of the very same challenges that make resilience so necessary to leadership. Resilient organizations do not escape adversity and disruptive change, but the more resilient the organization, the more challenges look like opportunities. As you will see in the final chapter of this book, resilient leaders do not shy away from creating necessary disruption. They get out front of adversity by engaging people in the system in challenging conversations that question assumptions and invite disorder.

KEY ASSUMPTIONS OF THE LEADERSHIP RESILIENCE MODEL

Drawing on research from the fields of leadership, change theory, organizational learning, emotional intelligence, resilience, and posttraumatic growth, the Leadership Resilience Model is founded on several key assumptions:

1. Relationships, resonance, and renewal shore up and enable leadership resilience.

   a. Leaders can't go it alone. Other people are important to their success.
   b. Optimism, vision, and compassion for oneself and others creates a powerful emotional force field that infuses hope, possibility, and a can-do perspective during times of disruptive change.
   c. Leaders need personal energy to sustain their focus and ability to bounce forward. They need to find what renews them, and they need to engage in those activities.

2. Leaders who continually nurture relationships, resonance, and renewal more easily activate and draw down stores of resilience when in the throes of disruptive change.

3. Leadership resilience is an inside-out job. Resilient leaders create resilient organizations.

4. It is helpful to look at the development of leadership resilience and what resilient leaders do. We can become more resilient ourselves through learning from those who have been resilient.

5. Resilience builds more resilience, out of which comes insight and wisdom to apply to future adversities.

6. Resilience is a discipline that must be practiced. Every moment offers a new chance to practice the actions of resilience.

BENEFITS OF THE LEADERSHIP RESILIENCE MODEL

The Leadership Resilience Model described in this book offers practitioners several benefits that make them more effective, balanced, and joyful leaders:

- It provides a way for you to act with *leadership resilience*—to bounce forward (not just simply return to a previous level of functioning) while you simultaneously create resilient organizations that breed leadership resilience in others.
- It is aspirational. It strives to convey ideal states of functioning and multiple pathways toward leadership resilience.
- It helps you assess your strengths and weaknesses in leadership resilience. It presents a desirable vision that you can compare yourself to and work toward.
- It asserts that you *can* become more resilient, and therefore, it poses both a challenge and a quest. Will you make up your mind to grow in resilience? Will you commit to a lifelong practice of leadership resilience?
- It will challenge other paradigms you might hold that are less helpful because they reinforce the idea that resilience is difficult and unattainable or that it is not something an individual can learn.
- It allows you to explore and talk about leadership resilience with interest, curiosity, and minimal defensiveness. You can look honestly at the concept of leadership resilience while reflecting on your own leadership resilience.
- It challenges you to overcome the limitations that constrain your leadership resilience and offers a blueprint for growth.

USING THE MODEL: A DISCIPLINED PRACTICE

With the hope that you gain all the benefits it offers both personally and professionally, I invite you to conceive of leadership resilience as a disciplined practice and not as a goal you need to achieve. Granted, as a practice, leadership resilience clearly is not a prepackaged single technique, magic bullet, or specific formula. It is unlikely that such a single solution exists. In the long run, however, treating leadership resilience as a practice is far more powerful and sustainable than any one technique could ever be. As a practice, you realize you have a lifetime to become more resilient. If you mess it up one day, you have the next day—really the next minute—to get back into the practice.

As a disciplined practice, you mindfully choose to take on the behaviors and guiding principles associated with bouncing forward. Kentucky superintendent Randy Poe suggests this is how leaders cultivate resilience. Poe says, "I've noticed this idea about what sets leaders apart from others. In large part it is the resiliency you build up from previous situations and then channel into the next experience. To do this, you have to have enough resilience to sustain you through the early challenges. If you don't, you won't make it. So you need to reflect on your experiences and be willing to learn about resilience so you can practice it."

Over time, leaders who practice resilience gain a resilient presence; they believe they are resilient, and others see them as resilient. Eventually, the behaviors of leadership resilience strengthen and then adapt with use, manifesting uniquely but consistently within your leadership context.

Part II

Enabling Capacities of Leadership Resilience

In this part of the book we explore the first part of the Leadership Resilience Model. This is the tetrahedron found in the center of the model anchored by the three leadership resilience enablers: Relationships, Resonance, and Renewal.

3 Relationships

*Surround Yourself
With Good Souls*

*The moment we cease to hold each other, the sea engulfs us and
the light goes out.*

—American writer James Baldwin (1924–1987)

In May 2011, a group of successful school leaders gathered together aboard the Queen Mary, now permanently anchored and operating as a boutique hotel at the docks in Long Beach, California, to participate in a focus group on the topic of resilience. When I asked these leaders to describe what helps them shoulder the stresses of their jobs, they all agreed: Relationships are key.

Researchers who study posttraumatic growth would not be surprised by what the educational leaders aboard the Queen Mary told me. Their studies show that people who come through adversity and ultimately feel stronger experience a heightened awareness of just how much the people in their lives, and the networks they belong to, mean to them. Apparently, successful educational leaders know from instinct and experience that linked networks of relationships make them more resilient. The lesson for novice and veteran educational leaders alike is profound: You must resist buying into the cliché that it is "lonely at the top." Even if your nature leans toward introversion, you must mindfully form and nurture relationships that sustain you and support you when adversity strikes. Don't settle for anything less.

A RELATIONSHIP INVENTORY

Before reading on, take a few moments to respond to the relationship inventory (to take the online version, visit www.WisdomOut.com) depicted in Exercise 3.1, which will provide you with objective feedback about your current state of "relationship." If you are reading this book as a leadership team, replace "I" with "We."

Instructions: Respond to each of the following statements quickly, providing your first impulse as the answer. If you are responding as a team, look at the average response or look at the amount of responses for each number in the range. A response of 10 is the strongest possible agreement, and 1 is the strongest possible disagreement. There are no correct answers.

Exercise 3.1   The Relationship Inventory

Statement	Strongly Disagree								Strongly Agree	
1. I have at least one close personal relationship where it is safe to be who I am, without any acting or pretending.	1	2	3	4	5	6	7	8	9	10
2. In my professional life, I have at least one relationship in which I can accept negative feedback without any threat to the relationship.	1	2	3	4	5	6	7	8	9	10
3. I can be very hurt by or disappointed with someone close to me, forgive him or her, and still maintain a close relationship.	1	2	3	4	5	6	7	8	9	10
4. When I hear other people speak with contempt about someone close to them, it makes me very uncomfortable.	1	2	3	4	5	6	7	8	9	10

Statement	Strongly Disagree									Strongly Agree
5. When I feel like a failure, I know someone I can talk to who will not judge me as a failure.	1	2	3	4	5	6	7	8	9	10
6. I can recall a conversation within the past couple of weeks in which I simply listened to the other person without interruption.	1	2	3	4	5	6	7	8	9	10
7. My closest colleagues at work know that they can occasionally blow off steam with me and that I will forgive them, even if they are a little bit out of control.	1	2	3	4	5	6	7	8	9	10
8. Some of my closet relationships are with people who give me candid advice, even when their candor hurts a little bit.	1	2	3	4	5	6	7	8	9	10
9. I can almost always think of something encouraging and nice to say to other people.	1	2	3	4	5	6	7	8	9	10
10. I have personally expressed gratitude to a person close to me at least once in the past week.	1	2	3	4	5	6	7	8	9	10

Total score: _____

Interpreting Your Score

Where do highly resilient people tend to score on the Relationship Inventory? Leaders who take the online version of the Relationship Inventory, and who also rate themselves high on happiness and meaningful work, score most often in the range of 71–100.

If You Score in the Range of 10–40: You claim to embrace a rugged individualism, but the reality is that yours is a sad, lonely, and difficult life. You perceive the people around you as being dense, difficult, and corrupt; they disappoint you at every turn. Sometimes you'd like to confide in someone, but if you took that risk, your partner might leave you, your friends would make fun of you, and your colleagues at work would use it against you. So you never risk being authentic. As a result of your isolation, your emotional and physical health may be suffering.

If You Score in the Range of 41–70: You consider yourself "nobody's fool." Several times you have given friends and colleagues the benefit of the doubt, and you've been burned. Up to a point, you are supportive, accepting, and nonjudgmental, but after a while it feels as if you're the only one doing the work in these relationships, and it's just not fair that you bear the burden of sustaining them. When it comes to new relationships at work and in your personal life, you're really on the fence. You often take a "wait and see" approach before you decide who to accept, appreciate, and trust. In summary, when it comes to relationships you are cautious. On occasion, relationships are a struggle for you. This usually has to do with the perception you hold that others have let you down. You can improve in relationships by being more clear and specific about what you are trying to accomplish and what you need from others to be successful. Remember, people cannot read your mind, so you must be willing to ask for help and show gratitude for help received.

If You Score in the Range of 71–100: You may not have thousands of friends, but you are very fortunate to have people in your personal and professional life who are true friends. You can confide in them and they in you. You attract these people because you too are a true friend, giving time, acceptance, and gratitude to others. If you scored in the 90s, then you are living by the Platinum Rule, giving more to others than you expect them to give to you. When you need their support, these supportive relationships will be there for you. The liability for you is that other less resilient people (who do not accomplish goals in their own work and life) may take advantage of you. This means that to be even more resilient as a leader, you need to give yourself permission to extend your energy to those relationships that are reciprocal and trustworthy and cut ties with those that diminish your ability to accomplish great things.

Reflection

Take a moment to reflect on the results of your Relationship Inventory.

My Relationship Inventory Score is: _____

Highlight key insights from the score interpretation you received. What sounds "right" to you? What seems off? What goals do you want to set for yourself or for your team?

_____

_____

_____

_____

_____

_____

HOW RELATIONSHIPS MAKE US RESILIENT

Castaway, starring Tom Hanks, is one of my favorite movies. In the film, Hanks is Chuck Noland, the lone survivor of a FedEx plane crash. Early in the film, a large box from the plane's cargo washes up on the island where Noland has found refuge. Noland opens the box with a knife, slicing his hand in the process. Still bleeding, Noland lifts out a volleyball made by the Wilson athletic company, leaving a bloody handprint that reminds him of a head with crazy-looking hair. In a moment of playfulness, given the severity of his situation, he draws in eyes, nose, and a mouth and names the ball "Wilson." As unusual as a relationship between a person and volleyball might be, Wilson is Noland's constant companion. When Noland figures out how to make a fire, Wilson is there. When Noland catches his first fish and enjoys his first real meal since washing up on the island, Wilson "watches" by the fire. And when Noland builds the raft that eventually takes him back out to sea in search of rescue, Wilson is there too. With Wilson by his side, Chuck Noland is able to take necessary action in order to survive. Wilson gave Noland courage.

Relationships Give Us Courage

As presented in Chapter 1, the hardships that confront educational leaders are neither rare nor unusual. Any day, anything can happen and as the wonderful Beatles song goes, we get by with a little help from our friends. Dependable networks of relationships are sources of courage; they give leaders confidence to move forward when they would rather stay in bed.

When Alyce, a former superintendent in the northwest, fought a decision made by the school board to exercise eminent domain in order to legally take over and demolish houses in a low-income neighborhood and make room for a new facility, she found herself at the center of a firestorm that included personal threats and attacks against her professional judgment. "The board thought these stakeholders were too disorganized to resist. Well, they were wrong, and when people began to speak up, I advocated for the community. Someone needed to make sure their voices were heard."

In the months that followed, Alyce was denigrated in the local newspapers. The same day the local paper published a particularly scathing letter to the editor, Alyce had to attend an evening event in the city. Feeling self-conscious and vulnerable, her plan was to eat one hors d'oeuvre and leave. "But then I felt an arm around my shoulder. It was the local police chief who told me I was doing a wonderful job. He said he watches community leaders and how they do things and he told me I had his support." This simple gesture from the police chief made all the difference to Alyce. She said, "He gave me courage to continue on the path I was on. Eventually, the board stood down and different decisions were made."

Relationships Promote Emotional and Physiological Well-Being

It turns out that the relationships that form your networks and give you courage also sustain your heart and mind. They promote good physical and mental health, which keeps you living longer and with sharper cognitive faculties (Jetten, Haslam, Alexander, & Branscombe, 2009; Ozbay et al., 2007).

For most people, close relationships are a source of happiness and comfort. They provide safe harbor from life's troubles. In their book *Loneliness: Human Nature and the Need for Social Connection* (2008), John Cacioppo and William Patrick write about the impact of prolonged loneliness on individuals and society. They suggest that connections with other people contribute to a person's ability to think, exert will power, persevere during tough times, and regulate emotions. And in the book titled *Bowling Alone: The Collapse and Revival of American Community* (2000), Robert Putnam writes, "As a rough rule of thumb, if you belong to no groups but decide to belong to one, you cut your risk of dying over the next year in half " (p. 331).

Relationships, however, do more than strengthen us emotionally. New findings indicate they also improve our physiological well-being. For example, social neuroscience experts Cacioppo and Patrick found that loneliness could have as detrimental an impact on a person's health as obesity or smoking. Loving relationships that ward off loneliness, on the other hand, can positively reduce several health problems including cardiovascular disease (Lynch, 2000). Other researchers found that having friends appears to increase immune system responses to flu shots in college students, while the lack of social connections reduces the benefits of exercise. (Zolli & Healy 2012). Zolli and Healy sum up the impact of relationships on personal well-being when they write, "Social isolation is not just bad for our psychological well-being. It appears to leave its trace at the cellular level" (p. 130).

WHO ARE YOUR WILSONS?

The odd but life-saving friendship we see between Wilson and Noland in the film *Castaway* provides a poignant example of the importance of relationships. And as the educational leaders aboard the Queen Mary told me, relationships allow us to be better and do better. They give us courage and fortitude. Every day, educational leaders must respond to challenges with resilience. And they can't do it alone. These leaders need to ask themselves, "Who are my Wilsons?" Equally important, they must also ask, "Whose 'Wilson List' am I on?"

"Relationship" has to do with the process leaders use to bond with and bridge people inside and outside the organization, who form valuable networks that generate social capital (Knoke, 1999; Nahapiet & Ghoshal, 1998).

Social capital can include resources, introductions to the "right" people, friendship, and love. When leaders leverage their networks in service of strategic goals that accomplish meaningful work, they influence the entire organization (Ibarra & Hunter, 2007).

Relationships That Provide Love

Some relationships provide love. *Late Bloomers* is a Swiss film about 80-year-old Marta, a former seamstress who decides, in spite of interference from her stuffy son and neighbors, to turn her late husband's grocery store into a racy and elegant lingerie shop. Lucky for Marta, she has four friends, including Lisi, who stand by her and will not let her give up. At one turning point in the film, Marta's son ransacks and closes her shop. That's when beautiful and flamboyant Lisi, who is frequently scorned and ridiculed by people in the village herself, encourages Marta to carry on. Marta gratefully tells her friend, "Lisi, you are such a good soul."

Veteran educational leader Carmen Franco told me, "It is important for leaders to follow negative experiences with positive experiences. If they don't, they risk inaction; they may not get up again. You need someone in your life who has your back. Leaders who are truly alone may not make it." Like Marta, resilient leaders have "good souls" in their lives who unconditionally love them and believe in them. These networks of family members, friends, and coworkers believe that you can accomplish anything you put your mind to. They are always there to listen and reflect back to you, your dearest dreams. Because these networks of people who love you expect you to succeed, they ask questions that point you toward your goals and might even scold you if you waver in your self-confidence.

James, a high school principal whose job was eliminated after a district consolidation, describes what it means to have a network of people who love you. "When I lost my job I felt ashamed," he said. "The superintendent made the decision to keep the other principal and let me go. It was a hard time for me because it felt so personal." James felt a wide range of emotions that immobilized him for a while. "I went from being principal and having a lot of responsibility and things to do, to sitting in my condo with nothing but my worries. The first thing I had to do, it turns out, was admit to myself that this was a hard time. Once I did that, I was able to ask others for help. It was my friends who helped me get my resume in order and get ready to go on job interviews. They told me I could do it. They restored my confidence."

Relationships That Support You With Resources

Leaders gain strength for themselves and for their school communities when they petition their network of relationships for support. I know of no other educational leader with better connections than Sister Marianella, who recently retired after serving 22 years as principal of St. Mary's Catholic School in Albuquerque, New Mexico. After so many years at the same school, Sister Nella, as she is known to all, has wonderful stories to tell about the students whom she calls her "Love Doves." But my favorite Sister Nella stories have to do with the many occasions that she petitioned a little-known saint named "Expedite" to ask for needed resources in the school. Sister Nella's introduction to Saint Expedite came when she was still in the convent and her Mother Superior asked them all to pray for a "deep freeze," one of those big old freezers that people sometimes keep in their basement or garage to store surplus frozen food. Back in those days, says Sister Nella, deep freezes were not all that common. So imagine how stunning it must have been when the next morning after their prayers, a man knocked on the convent door and asked if the nuns could use a deep freeze—he had one to give them if they would take it off his hands.

Over the years, Sister Nella and Saint Expedite became good friends. On one memorable occasion, as she and her St. Mary's office staff were pondering where to get $25,000 to pay for carpets in the preschool rooms, a community member knocked on the door and handed Sister Nella an envelope that he said contained a donation. Nella's impeccable manners prevented her from opening it in the moment, but grateful for any donation she thanked the gentleman profusely and he went on his way. What Sister Nella found in the envelope astonished the office staff who witnessed the entire exchange: It was a check for $25,000. On yet another occasion, Sister Nella told a generous donor that the school sure could use an art room. When Sister Nella told the donor the art room would cost $100,000, she received a check just a few cents shy. (The faculty passed a hat and came up with the remaining 56 cents or so.)

These are just three of the many Saint Expedite stories Sister Nella has to tell. The lesson all leaders need to take from Sister Nella, no matter what your spiritual or religious inclinations, is that good work attracts support, sometimes from surprising sources, as long as you make your needs known and ask for what you need.

Resilient leaders recognize a bountiful universe, but they also do the good and difficult work needed to draw support for their cause. Leaders who nurture their networks when things are going well can draw on them in times of need. In Sister Nella's case, she often received exactly what she prayed for. Sometimes, however, what leaders need in order to carry on comes in the form of skills, information, or mentoring. For example, one elementary principal named Carol, who was not an experienced grant writer, was told she had to produce a winning proposal in order to secure the extra books the teachers needed for their classroom libraries. Nervous that she would not be successful, Carol gratefully met with Bill, an acquaintance from one her business networks, who regularly wrote grants to run his nonprofit organization.

Bill reviewed Carol's proposal before she submitted it and suggested crucial revisions that won Carol's school the grant funds they sought.

Carol was smart to connect with someone from her network who possessed superb grant proposal writing skills and was willing to be of support to her. But sometimes leaders don't know the right people to turn to. In these cases, it is important to *know people who know the right people.*

Relationships That Open Doors

Leaders who shy away from "politics" put their resilience and the resilience of their organizations at peril. The truth is, all businesses, including the business of education, *is* political, in the best sense of the word, and much of what happens in the world happens through the amazing connections people have with each other (Sanders, 2002).

Bouncing forward is an enormous challenge without support and resources from others who help you stay on point during times of disruptive change. Claire's story provides an example. When Claire's district faced a storm of budget reductions, and cut the after-school activity program, parents in this primarily blue-collar community were crushed. How would they provide quality care for their children while they were at work? Claire, who served on several community boards and committees, knew that a number of them were looking for ways to reduce operational costs in the programs they ran for school-aged children. She made a few calls and put together a dialogue for all parties to come together to discuss how they could collaborate. In the end, Claire's district provided facilities for a number of community organizations to operate high-quality after-school programs for the students in her district.

In the context of leading in education, "politics" involves connecting with other leaders, constituencies, and enterprises from diverse segments of the community and knitting together networks of support in service of the purpose of the organization. Leaders who are serious about success, but squeamish about networking, must learn to make connections that matter (Baber & Waymon, 2007). When they do, these leaders realize that networks of support are created not through unseemly schmoozing, but through hard work and sincere interactions.

Oklahoma superintendent Lloyd Snow says that one way senior leaders create resilience is by being involved in the community. At the superintendent level, Snow explains, "If you are engaged in the civic clubs and the community, you can make it. I am or have been on the board of directors of almost all the civic clubs and the chamber of commerce. It is time consuming but if I'm not giving these groups constant updates and reports, I'm missing the chance to tell our story, and if that happens, they do not know how they can be of support to us when we need it."

Jan, a principal in a West Coast school district, also networks in her school community. Jan says, "Even though my superintendent takes his role in the community very seriously, I also get out and connect with people. After all, I live here, I shop here, and my kids go to school here. I just make sure my superintendent knows what committees I'm on, and I also make sure I listen a lot and not say things to accidently undermine what the superintendent is saying about our schools. It adds an extra responsibility, but it is still important for me to participate."

BEWARE OF NON-RESILIENT INDIVIDUALS

As open to others as resilient leaders are, they are not indiscriminate when deciding on whom they will spend their energy. Resilient leaders do not choose to spend an enormous amount of energy on single individuals who are strengthened by attention for behavior that weakens others. In work and in life, individuals who indulge in self-serving behaviors that undermine good work and positive change also undermine leadership resilience. These individuals might create a lot of noise in the system, but they are usually non-productive in their own work and lives, thus, they are non-resilient.

For example, "Lynn," who is the head of professional development in a regional agency, put an enormous amount of her staff's time and energy into developing a cutting-edge leadership academy to serve the districts in their consortium. Amidst a fair amount of pomp and bluster, the superintendent of the largest district, "Kris" insisted on certain allowances and adaptations to the program in order to meet the unique needs of her district. She also insisted on priority enrollment to the program, claiming the first two academies for her district alone. Lynn and her team at the regional agency did their best to accommodate Kris, even though it delayed implementation of the program and put smaller districts at a disadvantage. Finally, when the leadership academy was to launch, without providing explanation, Kris cancelled both of the academies she had agreed to. In addition, she seemed oblivious to the fact that the regional agency now had to scramble to fill the vacant slots that she initially claimed. Moreover, Kris did not seem to know or care when the leaders in her organization caught wind of the incident and lamented the loss of a quality leadership academy. She just blustered on to the next big idea.

Although Kris fancied herself as a dynamic and assertive leader who went after resources and support for her district, she neglected to see that she followed through on very few commitments and therefore accomplished very little. She also neglected to notice the battered relationships she left behind. Meanwhile, Lynn and her staff at the consortium learned a valuable lesson: Energy spent on non-resilient individuals is energy unwisely spent.

While we should have compassion for those who are non-resilient, we also must recognize them and employ strategies to minimize their power to undermine progress and good work. If you cannot eliminate the need to work with or rely on these people at all, ways to mitigate the impact of non-resilient individuals include securing clear and written agreements, identifying shorter milestones, employing the use of dependent flowcharts (where one thing must be accomplished before the next thing can occur), limiting their involvement in and responsibility for critical outcomes, setting up contingencies, and building in redundancies and simultaneous efforts that mitigate the fall-out when the non-resilient individual lets you down.

CHARACTERISTICS OF NON-RESILIENCY (IN OTHERS OR IN YOURSELF)

- Not achieving goals
- Not following through on agreements
- Making commitments in order to "look good" to others in the moment, but not with an intention to follow through
- A lack of grit when it comes to following through or following up on nitty-gritty details
- Sloppy work when it comes down to unglamorous but required tasks
- Blustery beginnings that fizzle
- A wake of strained and fractured relationships with others
- Other people do not want to collaborate with them or count on them
- Being a gossip monger
- Taking credit for the work of others

Resilient leaders do not accomplish great things by wasting energy on people and programs that hinder and halt positive change for a greater good. Resilient leaders know where they can make the greatest difference, and they choose to spend their energy where they can have an impact.

CULTIVATING THE LEADERSHIP RESILIENCE-ENABLER "RELATIONSHIPS"

In many cases, the lack of reliable networks is the root cause of a leader's inability to mobilize support for initiatives when facing resistance. Even leaders with undeniably clear and compelling visions that have the greater good at heart, can find themselves stunned to learn they do not have support from key individuals in their lives and in the system.

Not surprisingly, resilient leaders have a knack for cultivating important relationships in service of their organizations (Fullan, 2008). Anita Johnson, who is the executive director of the National Center for Education Research and Technology, says leaders must analyze goals from a systemic perspective and identify the crucial relationships necessary for success. Then, they must take steps to build relationships that provide the right support. As an example, Johnson told me, "Let's say you believe it is important that every student have a computer. Well, you can't just go off and write the purchase order for computers. You have to have been building relationships with people who are critical to the successful implementation of computers, way in advance of their actual purchase."

Leaders who develop a knack for connecting with people and groups in order to gain access to support and resources they lack through their own connections, develop a number of networking competencies—what Lloyd Snow calls "chemistry"—for getting people to come together for school improvement. To create chemistry for support, leaders need to hone several skills that promote relationships:

1. **Be mindful about what you say.** Have the courage to speak respectfully even about hot topics. But be mindful about what you say and how you say it. Ask yourself if the words you are about to speak moves people closer together or further apart.

2. **Be open.** Inquire into differing perspectives and know when to "agree to disagree."

3. **Persist in helping people understand the facts.** Be fluent and accurate in expressing your successes and challenges. Point out existing resources and enumerate gaps in resources. Provide information at every opportunity. Engage candidly about what you need from others, and what you do not want or need.

4. **Reflect the best of what other people and groups do, back to them.** Point out and celebrate what people and other groups do well and help them challenge learned helplessness. This will help them build their resilience capacity, which makes everyone stronger.

5. **Facilitate connections.** Listen and learn the needs of other groups in the network and connect them with each other. Hone your ability to see connections systemically and broker relationships between groups.

6. **Treat people as if they matter.** Stop and interact with people, even those who appear to lack resources for your cause. Not only might they be delightful people to know, but they may have other

connections that can be of aid to you down the road. Assume people want to help. Reciprocate sincerely when people need your support and when you are able to give it.

7. **Articulate the current state of your organization compared to the ideal vision, and do so regularly, repeatedly, and consistently.** Two things mobilize people to action: absolute dissatisfaction with the current situation and having a vision of something far better. When you describe both the current state and the vision of your organization to others, they see both the opportunities and the challenges and more ways to be of support. When you talk about your vision, New York superintendent Robert Dubik reminds you that authenticity counts. He says that leaders who are absolutely committed to their work have little problem being genuine: "People might get tired of hearing the same message about your vision over and over again, but they begin to understand that you are sincere. You are not self-serving."

8. **Caretake your reputation.** The best way to do this is to follow through on your commitments and do everything you undertake as well as you can.

9. **Share your aspirational, big ideas—even those that are "crazy" or seem impossible.** Progress occurs when good ideas receive the energy they need to move to the next level. Resilient leaders ensure progress through skillful advocacy of big ideas that capture the passion of their networks, both inside and outside the organization.

10. **Help people learn.** Learning is the business we are in, after all! Leaders who help others learn, empower them, and make them stronger and more able to reciprocate when they are in need. For example, one of my clients invited community business partners to attend a leadership coaching academy I ran for them. In this model, school leaders partnered with leaders from the community to learn coaching skills and to coach each other through important projects. The outcome was powerful and went a long way to forge school and community relations. Both parties came away with keen insight into the work of the other and even felt invested in the success of each other's projects.

11. **Coach someone who needs to think through an important challenge.** Resilient leaders are coaching leaders who build the capacity for leadership in others. Leaders who coach know that listening builds relationships. Therefore, resist giving advice and resist giving *your* answer to the problem. Instead, just listen.

12. **Follow up with the people you supervise.** Lisa Harris, a specialist for foreign language with the Virginia Department of Education who has served on several teacher-evaluation review boards, says that the number one problem is administrators who tell teachers what they need to learn and do to improve but then fail to hold regular coaching conversations with them to reflect on new learning and plan for using it. Harris says, "These administrators fail to sustain a relationship with teachers. They don't realize that it is not enough to tell teachers what to do—they also have to follow up with them." Evaluators who coach their direct reports create powerful relationships where any topic can come up and any challenge can be faced.

RESILIENCE AS A SOCIAL IDENTITY

When educational leaders connect to others in the face of loss, they also establish a precedent for *how* to connect with each other when facing challenges in the future. During times of challenge, your leadership resilience can strengthen the networks you belong to.

Michigan superintendent Mark Bielang and his leadership team began one school year with the recent death of a colleague on their minds. Rather than plow through the opening agenda he had planned, Bielang put it aside and made time simply for his team to talk about how they felt and what they were thinking. Bielang said, "Doing this deepened our relationships with one another and created more understanding about other things going on in our lives and work."

Efficacy certainly is a by-product of handling challenges well. When individuals and groups gain awareness about *how* they are effective, they are galvanized to handle whatever comes their way. More importantly, however, their identity transforms: They step more fully into *being* people and teams known for the way they handle challenges. Bielang told me, "Once we experienced the growth that came from talking together, our leadership team emerged with a greater sense of self-confidence and organizational confidence, which we use to face other important matters. Just recently, in fact, we had an honest conversation about what creates trust and what undermines trust in our district. We might not have had that conversation before we experienced ourselves as able to have tough conversations."

Although retired now, Jody Leinenwever is another leader whose visible resilience made her a role model for many and who recognized her responsibility to embrace a resilient identity. When I met and worked with Leinenwever in the Pendergast School District in Arizona, she already had the reputation of a trailblazer. Early in her career she was one of the first women in the area to hold a senior leadership position. At conferences and in meetings, other women would approach her and ask for advice about their career paths. At the same time Leinenwever was opening doors for herself and others, she was also diagnosed with a slow-growing, benign brain tumor that she lives with to this day. Although not everyone knew about her medical condition, some did, and this knowledge made them more courageous in their own lives. In Leinenwever they saw a resilient leader who could do more than teach them the ropes; she could teach them to overcome anything that undermined their well-being.

BE A GOOD SOUL

Just as you have good souls in your life who love you, provide you with resources, and open doors for you during times of adversity, you increase resiliency for all when you are a "good soul" to others. Alyce, the superintendent who faced personal attacks when she supported vulnerable stakeholders with homes marked for take-over through eminent domain, says, "When that police chief put his arm around my shoulder, it was a protective gesture that was also incredibly encouraging. As I went on in my career I became a leader who did this for others; I knew how much it mattered."

SUMMARY

Relationships are good for you emotionally and physiologically. They give you courage, and they make you stronger especially during times of disruptive change. When adversity strikes, your networks of relationships will want to be of support, but only if you make them a priority when life is smooth and calm. Resilient leaders look to the vision, mission, and prioritized strategies of their organizations, and they identify the relationships likely to come into play. Then, resilient leaders will prioritize these relationships and take steps to sincerely grow them.

ACTIVITIES AND QUESTIONS FOR
STUDY GROUPS AND TEAMS

1. People come into our lives to teach us, to challenge us, to support us, and to help us grow. Either working alone or as a team, make a list of the people and organizations that are new to you in your work and life. These individuals may be new faculty and staff, new bosses, new board members, new students, or new community groups. They could be new partnerships, new liaisons, or new advisers. Reflect on what these individuals bring to your organization at this time and what they need from you. Reflect on what you and your organization could learn from them.

2. Think about the 10 most important people in your life. How often do you initiate interactions with them where you ask them what they are working on and what their latest successes have been? Out of these 10, who will you check in with in the next month?

3. What do you have to give to others? Do you have expertise and knowledge that a colleague needs? Who needs your talents and skills in order to accomplish their important work and serve the goals of the organization?

4. Who needs you to listen to them as they process something important or troublesome in their life or work? What do you wish someone would listen to you about?

5. What do you need to learn or have from someone else that would allow you to lead through a specific challenge? Who do you know whom you can ask for help with this?

6. Who do you need to thank for what they have given you or taught to you or shown to you through their example? Thank five people every day and when you do, tell them specifically what you are grateful for. Example: "When you showed me how you set up the timeline for that project, I had a breakthrough on the project I am working on. Thank you for sharing your expertise with me."

7. Have you lost important relationships in your life either with a colleague or family member? How did it happen? On the other hand, have you repaired an important relationship in your life? What actions did you take to do this?

8. What do you love about the work you do? What specifically do you love about the tasks, the processes, and the relationships involved in your work?

9. Who inspires you? Who do you inspire? Who would love for you to notice them, and what would that allow them to do or how would they think differently about themselves?

10. How good are you at meeting your obligations and commitment to others? Do you follow through on promises? Do others consider you or your team trustworthy? Can you be counted on?

11. Who loves you, and who do you love? What does this tell you about yourself? Try to describe in words what you mean to others.

4 Resonance

Martin Luther King didn't become famous saying, "I have a complaint."

—Van Jones

A great way to get people talking about resonance is to ask them to describe a person they know who is really great to be around—someone who not only positively changes the atmosphere in the room when they walk in the door, but who also has the ability to motivate others to action. Then ask them to talk about what they have done in their own life and work that they attribute to the inspiration and energy they receive from interacting with this person. This conversation, when held among colleagues, surfaces relatable stories that make resonance easy to understand. I'll begin by telling you about two educators I know who always bring out the best in me.

Back in the late 1990s at the Pendergast School District in the west valley of Phoenix, I had the privilege of working with and being mentored by superintendent Ron Richards and assistant superintendent of Human Resources, Jody Leinenwever. Richards and Leinenwever are the sort of leaders who light up a room the minute they enter it. Within minutes of meeting them, you realize you are in the presence of an extraordinary pair. As experts in interest-based bargaining, Richards and Leinenwever have a way of putting people at ease, even in difficult situations. They use the skills they learned over the years to listen deeply, ask questions that lead to important conversations, and seek to understand the needs of every person. They infuse people with hope and possibility, and somehow they inspire people to interact from their best selves. As a result, they motivate individuals and teams to tackle difficult issues and come up with solutions that serve a greater good.

Richards and Leinenwever possess a megadose of what we've come to know as *emotional resonance,* which is also an essential enabler of leadership resilience. The more you have cultivated the ability to interact with people from an emotionally resonant stance, the more practiced and empowered you are to do so during times of adversity. Resonance ignites people with hope, optimism, and commitment and provides leaders with an uncommon knack for rallying the organization during times of disruptive change.

In the foreword of Boyatzis and McKee's book *Resonant Leadership: Renewing Yourself and Connecting With Others Through Mindfulness, Hope, and Compassion* (2005), Daniel Goleman explains that emotionally resonant leaders are those who are self-aware, socially aware, and self-motivated. Goleman writes that these individuals are "able to somehow radiate that positivity, igniting and mobilizing positive attitudes in those around them." To understand the practical application of resonance you only have to recall those times when you've said about someone, "I like her vibe!" or "I love working with him; he has good energy," or "She has great mojo and always gets things done—of course I'll help her out." These comments are markers for resonance; they signal the favorable emotional energy you detect in those who compel *you* to action.

A RESONANCE INVENTORY

Before reading on, take a few moments to respond to the Resonance Inventory (to take the online version, please visit www.WisdomOut.com) depicted in Exercise 4.1, which will provide you with objective feedback about your current state of "resonance." If you are reading this book as a leadership team, replace "I" with "We."

Instructions: Respond to each of the following statements quickly, providing your first impulse as the answer. If you are responding as a team, look at the average response or look at the amount of responses for each number in the range. A response of 10 is the strongest possible agreement, and 1 is the strongest possible disagreement. There are no correct answers.

Exercise 4.1 The Resonance Inventory

Statement	Strongly Disagree									Strongly Agree
1. When I see colleagues I do not know well or a complete stranger crying, it makes me uncomfortable. The last thing I wanted to know is the details of another person's life. They may have problems, but they certainly do not involve me.	1	2	3	4	5	6	7	8	9	10
2. Whenever I see a group of people laughing, it makes me worry that either I didn't get the joke or perhaps that they are secretly laughing at me. I never join in the laughter, but I either avoid the situation entirely or suggest that we've got serious work to do and we had better get to it.	1	2	3	4	5	6	7	8	9	10
3. When I notice a friend, family member, or colleague who is clearly fearful, I try to help them snap out of it. "Hey," I tell them, "you're not a kid, and there are no dragons under the bed anymore!" If they pull this fear act too often, I tell them to grow up and start acting their age. In fact, it's unsettling to me when people around me show fear.	1	2	3	4	5	6	7	8	9	10
4. When I see someone taking pride in something minuscule—like thinking that their grandkid is the only cute baby in the world—I just tune it out. "Okay. Your kid's on the honor roll and is *really, really* gifted—and so are you. So can we get back to work now?"	1	2	3	4	5	6	7	8	9	10
5. When colleagues or friends are perpetually happy, it makes me wonder about them. These are serious times, and serious people don't get into good moods unless they are in active denial. They must not watch the news, and they certainly don't know what's going on in our organization, or they would be a bit more sober and take life more seriously. Their good moods make me question their judgment and grip on reality.	1	2	3	4	5	6	7	8	9	10
6. I secretly admire some leaders whom other people seem to despise. They are tough, but I think they are fair. When they chew somebody out publicly, they say out loud what I think—and what everybody thinks but just won't say.	1	2	3	4	5	6	7	8	9	10
7. My siblings, family, and close friends know not to intrude too much on my personal feelings. They know I don't appreciate anybody else, no matter how close they may be, asking me about how I feel about things.	1	2	3	4	5	6	7	8	9	10
8. If a colleague gives a presentation and starts to choke up at the end when he or she talks about how important the topic is to him or her or to the organization, I find it embarrassing and totally unprofessional.	1	2	3	4	5	6	7	8	9	10
9. If I see a colleague or friend get too emotional, I try to help them out by lightening up the mood and changing the subject.	1	2	3	4	5	6	7	8	9	10
10. It hardly ever happens, but on those very rare occasions when my emotions get the better of me, I just excuse myself. I'd much rather be alone than around family, friends, or colleagues when I'm emotional.	1	2	3	4	5	6	7	8	9	10

Total score: _____

Interpreting Your Score

Where do highly resilient people tend to score on the Resonance Inventory? Leaders who take the online version of the Resonance Inventory, and who also rate themselves high on happiness and meaningful work, score most often in the range of 10–40.

If You Score in the Range of 10–40: Although at times it seems that you wear your heart on your sleeve, you usually have the ability to frame your strong emotions and the emotions of others in ways that people around you perceive as helpful, empathetic, and compassionate. You likely have a strong ability to set an emotional tone for the organization that helps people move forward. For example, when grieving would help, you are not too embarrassed or too shy to display sadness. When inspired action and creativity are needed, you are the first one to display hope and excitement. You have a knack for contextualizing your emotions in the mission and vision of the group in ways that others find credible and authentic. Your social-emotional awareness makes you a helpful coach for your colleagues and peers. Usually, you are able to maintain your equanimity in the company of those in distress without being taken advantage of by someone who uses emotional displays for the purpose of manipulation. The challenge for you when it comes to emotional intelligence is remaining productive and focused toward movement when your emotions or the emotions of others could take you off track. On occasion, you might also need to buffer yourself better from the affect of others' emotions on you.

If You Score in the Range of 41–70: Although you are aware of your emotions and how they effect others, you may appear to others to be too calculating in the emotions you decide to share with others and the emotions you decide to keep in check. While your ability to monitor and regulate your emotions is usually helpful, you may come across to others as being inauthentic in your emotional response. As a result, you may not be using your own emotional reality to inspire others to action. You can get better at this by contextualizing your emotions within the mission and vision of the team or organization. Show and tell others what you feel and how it connects to meaningful work. Do the same for others too. When the people around you display strong emotions, help them reframe them as calls to action and resilience.

If You Score in the Range of 71–100: It's almost always good to be rational—and you certainly are. It's sometimes good to be alone—and you probably are. But it's not helpful to be angry, sullen, cynical, distrustful, vengeful, spiteful, and full of regret. It may feel to you that the people around you are attempting to take advantage of you, manipulate you, and prey on your feelings. At times, however, it might occur to you that rationality alone is not the key to happiness. After all, lots of people know that the square of the hypotenuse is equal to the sum of the square of the two sides, and they are right. But being right is not always enough—you also need to connect with people at an emotional level.

Reflection

Take a moment to reflect on the results of your Resonance Inventory.

My Resonance Inventory Score is: _____

Highlight key insights from the score interpretation you received. What sounds "right" to you? What seems off? What goals do you want to set for yourself or for your team?

_____

_____

_____

_____

_____

_____

A FORCE FIELD OF POSITIVE ENERGY

Resonance is a force field of positive energy projected outward from one person, infusing those around them with hope, vision, and compassion (Boyatzis & McKee, 2005). Resonance also has a ripple effect; the positive emotions embedded in resonance are contagious, and the resonance of a single leader can set the tone for the entire organization. When adversity and disruptive change strikes, resilient leaders are never more resonant. They maintain their presence and keep their cool even when chaos swirls about them.

As with the other inventories provided to you in this book, the online version of the Resonance Inventory (that you completed in the exercise above), first asks participants to rate their level of happiness about their work and the extent to which they believe their work is meaningful to the organization. What I've found from analyzing the data is that the leaders who rate themselves high on both happiness and meaningful work fall in a range of resonance that reveals a high level of emotional interaction with others.

This range certainly is in opposition to the category at the other end of the scale where emotions are shunned in favor of "rational" hard data, but it is even left of the center range, where emotions and rationality are more balanced.

When I ask leaders who score on the more emotional side of the scale to give me details about their interactions, they emphasize the need to reign in their own emotions, especially those that are negative or overzealous, while they simultaneously accept and show compassion for the emotions of others. This mixture of self-awareness and openness to others is what it takes to keep people moving forward.

The key to harnessing strong emotions without becoming overwhelmed is in learning how to contextualize them—how to place them in the stories of specific students and other stakeholders and relate them to the mission and vision of the organization. Commenting on the research of neuroscientist Richard Davidson, who looks at different emotional styles that originate in the brain, Daniel Goleman implies that people who experience deeper emotions may even have an advantage over those who are less emotional, provided they find a way to communicate them. He says, "Some people experience their feelings quite intensely, some people quite shallowly. Those who have stronger feelings may be better able to authentically communicate them more powerfully—to move people" (2011, Kindle Location 365–367).

Here is a story to illustrate this point: I worked with "Susan," a superintendent who had strong feelings about recruiting principals with skills and experience in urban communities. When Susan passionately led a task force to champion the new recruitment process, she first encountered a great deal of resistance from principals who had been in the district long term and who interpreted her enthusiasm as criticism for their performance. The turning point came for Susan when she harnessed the collective voice of the task force—which included many veteran principals—and gave it eloquent expression. The resonant voice of the committee (rather than Susan's passionate yet sometimes strident approach) reduced the anxiety of the veteran principals and brought the focus back to what they could do together to recruit and develop leaders who were in tune with the school community.

HOW RESONANCE ENABLES RESILIENCE

Resonance is achieved when leaders positively drive the emotions of the workforce, allowing them to accomplish the good work of the organization even in the face of continual change and downright adversity. Dissonance, on the other hand, results when emotional securities are undermined (Goleman, Boyatzis, & McKee, 2004) and people become less able to accomplish goals. The more resonant you are as a leader, the more able you are to move others forward in the aftermath of change. In the words of

Resonant Leadership authors Boyatzis and McKee (2005), "Great leaders move us" (p. 1).

Emotional Intelligence and Emotional Brain Patterns

In large part, resonance depends on your emotional intelligence (EI)—especially your ability to manage your emotions and set the emotional tone for others. Goleman, who was trained as a psychologist at Harvard and was also a science writer for the *New York Times,* was the first person to bring emotional intelligence to the attention of contemporary audiences. Goleman frames his theory of emotional intelligence in the workplace, and he particularly elaborates on emotional intelligence as it applies to leadership (1998, 2004).

Goleman's EI model is made up of four domains: self-awareness, self-management, social awareness, and relationship management. Each domain is comprised of several competencies, some that have to do with being aware of emotions and how they are operating on people and the organization, and others that have to do with taking action to regulate those emotions for the good of themselves, others, and the organization (1998).

A BRIEF SUMMARY OF THE FOUR DOMAINS OF EMOTIONAL INTELLIGENCE

Domain 1: Self-Awareness. Leaders who are good in *self-awareness* can read their own emotions and recognize their impact on others. They also are aware of their own strengths and limits, and possess a solid sense of self-worth.

Domain 2: Self-Management. Leaders who are good in *self-management* keep their emotions in check, respond well to changing situations, have a personal drive to improve, take action when presented with opportunities, and are optimistic in their views.

Domain 3: Social Awareness. Leaders who are strong in *social awareness* notice the emotions of others and are sensitive to them. They also detect how emotions play out in the climate of the organization. They are politically astute and seek to meet the needs of others.

Domain 4: Relationship Management. Finally, leaders who are strong in *relationship management* use a compelling vision to inspire others and have a variety of strategies (such as coaching) to influence and develop people and teams. These leaders are skilled at leading change and at creating relationships that create solid backing for organizational change.

Emotional Styles

New research from neuroscientist Richard Davidson provides additional insight into emotional intelligence. In his book *The Emotional Life of Your Brain: How Its Unique Patterns Affect the Way You Think, Feel and Live— and How You Can Change Them* (2012), Davidson explains that his research arose out of two observations: first, that different people respond differently to life's trials, and second that the people he knows who go through life with equanimity all do something quite deliberate and mindful, like meditation, for example, to have that ability. In other words, these individuals were not always emotionally balanced all the time, but they became that way by taking advantage of neuroplasticity and providing themselves with experiences that reshaped the circuitry in their brain.

These two observations led Davidson to focus his research first on how the structure and neuroactivity of the brain creates different emotional styles in different people. Second, Davidson showed how practices that promote well-being (such as meditation) operate on the mind, which over time restructures the brain—in this case, of course, toward a style of functioning that is more level-headed, calm, and composed in the face of disruption. In his book, Davidson describes six emotional styles that people possess in combination, to various degrees:

1. **Resilience.** How rapidly or slowly you recover from adversity.

2. **Outlook.** How long positive emotions persist following a joyful event.

3. **Social Intuition.** The accuracy with which you detect nonverbal social cues from others.

4. **Context.** The extent to which you regulate your emotions according to the context.

5. **Self-Awareness.** Your awareness of your own bodily signals that constitute emotion.

6. **Attention.** The extent to which your attention is either focused or scattered.

Some people pick up on their emotions and the emotions of others very well and are relatively unflappable and recover quickly from distress. These individuals are more able to detect growing emotional dissonance in themselves and others and take steps to turn things around. Others are easily upset and take a long time to recover and seem to be unaware of emotional changes in themselves and others. Referencing Davidson's work, Goleman observes that the latter group also tends to be chronic worriers, thereby putting themselves in a state of continual emotional hijacking that generates stress and produces stress hormones that wreak havoc on emotional and physiological well-being (more about the effects of stress hormones in Chapter 5). Goleman says, "Given the many realistic stresses we face, those first two styles—being unflappable and capable of quick recovery—are the most effective in navigating the troubles of the world of work" (2011, Kindle Location 363–364).

The Responsibility to Become More Resonant

Setting a resonant tone is not easy work. Janine Hoke, director of Professional Growth and Development, observes that resonant leadership initially puts a lot on the back of the leader. "Leaders must take the first step," Hoke reflects. "They have to stay resonant even when others are not. When they tough it out, however, the tide starts to turn. Trust builds and people see that the vision is achievable. Then, other people in the system also begin to lead with resonance and now the leader is no longer alone. But the resonant leader, literally, sets the tone."

Challenging as it might be, leaders have a responsibility to increase their resonance for the simple fact that it makes others more resilient. In a study on leadership behavior and the effect it has on resilience in subordinates, for example, researchers at the University of Nebraska found that participants who exhibited greater resilience mentioned their leaders as a positive factor over participants who were less resilient (Harland, Harrison, Jones, & Reiter-Palmon, 2005). Another example of resilient leadership comes from remembering how Trudi Spierling, a beloved Washington State school principal who passed away in 2010, interacted with teachers and colleagues. I wrote about Spierling in 2012 (Allison et al., 2012) after I was fortunate to meet her at a Florida conference in 2009 and talk with her about leadership. She told me that after she got her cancer diagnosis, she became more aware of connecting with individuals from a positive emotional state that allows them to access their strengths and be inspired to continue to grow. She said, "Most of my real reflections since having cancer has been about how I will make my individual one-on-one conversations go well—where I can share with teachers what I love about what they are doing and where they need to grow. I think it will be easier for me now to have these conversations more directly, using words that inspire the best in each person I speak with." Spierling's emotional self-awareness allowed her to create resonant relationships with the people she led. Knowing this was a source of great comfort for her in her last year of life. What emotional force field do you wish to create in your organization?

The Challenge for Novice Leaders

The responsibility to become more resonant is especially required for new or novice leaders who are inexperienced in setting the emotional tone for an entire organization or team and who have not learned to quell the cocky needs of their ego. Robert Sutton makes this point in a post he wrote for the online *Bloomberg Businessweek* magazine (2008). Sutton, a Stanford University professor and author of the book *The No Asshole Rule,* tells of an amusing study conducted by researchers at Berkeley who found that given the opportunity, people with new leadership powers will "eat more cookies, chew with their mouths open and leave more crumbs." One inference we can make from the "cookie study" is that because they lack the vast array of leadership experiences that would cultivate emotional connections in their brains, and/or because they lack awareness for how their behavior affects others, new leaders may be low in a number of the emotional styles Davidson writes about, especially social intuition, context, and self-awareness.

Given that we now understand the contagious nature of emotions, and have ideas from neuroscientists about how we can reshape our brain patterns in order to behave with greater equanimity, only the most clueless of leaders would choose not to become more resonant.

Cultivating Resonance

The very real demands of leadership take their toll, making leaders less resonant or even dissonant in their interactions with others. Over time, a lack of positive resonance creates tension and distress in the organization. In a healthy economy where people have choices about where they work, persistent negative emotions—especially when the leader is the source of negativity—will drive people away. A fleeing workforce and the accompanying need to constantly recruit and train new employees undermines your ability to lead with resilience and undermines the resilience of the entire organization. In this section, I provide you with tactics for cultivating resonance—for making you more compassionate, hopeful, and mindful—and for transmitting those qualities throughout the organization.

Learn to Listen

Compassion is the act of understanding what people need and then feeling moved to take helpful and appropriate action on their behalf. In education, for example, leaders show compassion when they first take time to understand what stakeholders need to achieve goals and then they seek to provide the ways and means (e.g., professional development, time, tools, processes) to meet those needs.

Compassion is impossible, however, if you are not a good listener. Leaders who have not learned to listen—really listen—give the impression that they do not care, even when they do. Listening increases the chance that you will focus on the other person and the present moment without making assumptions and without acting out of your own history.

Good listeners defeat the bad habits that prevent them from *really* listening. Bad habits, such as interrupting, judging, giving advice, taking over, multitasking, and reacting to things that push your button, interfere with your ability to resonate compassion and hope. In addition to overcoming bad listening habits, leaders who listen well, listen in the moment and on behalf of the other person—not from the past and what MIT lecturer William Isaacs calls their "personal net of memories." In his groundbreaking book on dialogue, Isaacs writes, "To listen is to realize that much of our reaction to others comes from memory; it is stored reaction, not fresh response at all" (1999, p. 92). When you remove the net of your own memories and listen to people with a fresh mind, you successfully suspend the judgments and resistance that interferes with listening and which make you less compassionate.

Listening to Empower. Leaders who listen also empower others to uncover insights that move them to take action. Looked at this way, listening is actually a powerful leadership development strategy. When I teach leadership coaching skills, for example, 100% of the time participants are astonished to learn just how much it means to people when they simply and sincerely listen to them. These leaders are equally surprised and a little bit chagrined to realize just how poor they are at listening. At the end of a listening exercise I led with educational leaders in Zambia, for example, here is what they told me when I asked them what it felt like to be listened to without interruption, judgment, or resistance:

- "It felt like for once, I was able to hear myself think."
- "It felt like if I could keep talking, I would figure the whole thing out."
- "It felt like my coach really cared about me and what I was facing."
- "I realized that what I first thought was the issue really wasn't it at all."
- "I heard myself explain the problem I'm facing with greater clarity."
- "It felt like someone trusted me to know what to do."
- "It felt funny, but knowing I wasn't going to be interrupted, I was able to be more thoughtful about what I said."

Emily Dickinson is quoted as having written to a friend, "I felt it shelter to speak with you" (Wineapple, 2009, p. 216). Dickinson's words beautifully express the value of listening. When we listen people feel understood, they feel their ideas matter, they feel less isolated, and in the aftermath of disruptive change they are more likely to join leaders in creating new pathways toward excellence. Speaking of the power of listening as it relates to leadership coaching, Doreen Corrente, executive director of the Rhode Island Center for School Leadership (RICSL), says, "What was surprising to everyone was to learn how to use the simple skill of listening to empower people." In other words, said Corrente, "listening is a way to develop the whole culture."

Be Optimistic

Leaders who resonate optimism spread hope and a spirit of "can do" throughout the organization. Consider the incredible results achieved in high-poverty schools across the country where traditionally underserved students excel. Educational leaders who take the helm of struggling schools and districts are motivated toward success by a harsh reality: too many young people who may not make it in the world. These leaders cannot afford pessimism; they believe they can make a difference. If they did not, why on earth would they show up each day and devote themselves to turning things around?

Inspired by Harsh Truths. In the face of harsh realities and brutal truths, leaders who are resilient are optimistic but not naive—they are aware of the difficulties facing them. However, resilient leaders find negative data compelling. Instead of focusing cynically on what they cannot do, resilient leaders see what they can do. Rather than complain about what they want less of from others, resilient leaders describe what they want more of. Whereas pessimistic leaders use negative data as an excuse to throw up their hands, point fingers, and lose focus, the same appalling information inspires optimistic leaders to action.

In the *Renewal Coaching Fieldbook* (Allison et al., 2012), I write about Debbie Lee, who is director of Secondary Curriculum and Instruction in Waterloo, Iowa. Lee serendipitously came up with the term "brutiful data." Originally a slip of the tongue made while in conversation with colleagues as they were analyzing student achievement data, Lee immediately recognized the wisdom of the chance double entendre. If you know Lee, you know this level of optimism is characteristic. "Brutiful data" provides a perfect description of the unique combination of perspectives that leaders of sustainable change possess—yes, the data presents a brutal reality, but we can do something about it, which is beautiful. Lee is undeterred by harsh realities, especially when the well-being of students is at stake.

Celebrate Small Wins

Resonant leaders move others to action. Therefore, one way to determine your level of leadership resonance is to look at the organization's progress toward and eventual achievement of important goals. Progress toward the goals of the organization can be thought of as small wins. Small wins do not mean small goals; they are incremental gains in the direction you want to go. Where small wins occur, they reveal where the organization has traction and where it can leverage early gains into more significant gains.

Small wins are aided by a transparent and consistent approach to measure leadership performance. Anita Johnson, executive director of NCERT and whom you first met in Chapter 3, says it is especially important for superintendents to relate growth and progress to the goals that are linked to their evaluation and contract. In order to create resonance, however, and to inspire others to mobilize around the goals, Johnson says highly resilient leaders provide updates that explain and demonstrate the connections between seemingly unrelated work and crucial district priorities. This is especially true for superintendents, says Johnson, because almost all of their accomplishments depend on the work of other individuals and teams. Johnson told me, "The superintendent keeps the district moving forward by reporting gains made directly by them or by others, all the time. Every time something is put in motion or accomplished in service of a larger goal, the leader has to make the connection specific and explicit. The leader literally needs to say, 'this accomplishment is for goal number three' or 'this accomplishment is for goal number six.'"

Leaders who draw attention to small wins and who celebrate the people and the strategies that created them, infuse the organization with hope and faith that the vision is achievable. Celebrations of small wins also keep the minds of stakeholders focused on what matters and focused on what they *can do* to keep progress moving forward rather than what they fear they *cannot do.*

SMALL WINS

Here is a list of small wins to look for in education. What would you add to this list specific to your organization, classroom, or initiative?

- Celebrate closing in on a goal—narrowing a gap. Be specific about the percentage changes and include details about the tactics, resources, and people associated with the changes.
- Celebrate the "favorite mistakes"—those errors and blunders that create an upside of knowledge and insight, those "a-ha!" moments about how to refine and hone the next approach.
- Celebrate cultural artifacts that represent change. One example might be schedules of PLCs that show a trend toward collaboration. Another might be a data display of increasing graduation rates for typically underserved student groups—complete with photos and quotes from recent graduates.

(Continued)

(Continued)

Another might be the percentage of project-based learning presentations completed by students, which demonstrates a more integrated approach to instruction. And yet one more example might be the percentage of teachers who observe in their colleagues' classrooms, signaling a move toward more openness and trust.

- Celebrate behavioral wins. For example, if you want students reading at higher levels, celebrate the increase in number of books read. If you want students who are proficient in science, celebrate the percentage of students from diverse socioeconomic groups who are new to Odyssey of the Mind and to robotics competitions. If you want more students thinking critically, celebrate student membership in entrepreneur clubs.
- Celebrate the number or percentage of employees who learned something new and shared it with a wider audience.
- Extend and increase goals and then celebrate the new challenge.
- Peter Senge wrote, "Truly creative people use the gap between vision and current reality to generate energy for change" (1990, p. 153). Therefore, celebrate the number of people who take new action in response to the presentation of a challenging vision. Take surveys once in a while asking "on a scale of 1–5, with 1 being low and 5 being high, are your actions leading to the organizational vision?"
- Celebrate craftsmanship—find the teachers who teach challenging standards very well and create opportunities for others to witness them teach and go back to their own classrooms and do the same.

Remember That You Matter to Others

Although neuroscientists have shown that the limbic system is open and that emotions are contagious, spreading from one person to another, many leaders fail to act on this knowledge. They go about their workday going from one task to the next without noting just how much they mean to the people around them and the effect they have on them. They miss opportunities to connect with and inspire the people they lead.

In order to increase your resonance, it is important for you to be mindful of your connection to others and how much you mean to the people in your personal and professional life. Being mindful that your words, demeanor, and emotions make a difference for others makes you humble and tender. When you are mindful about how much you mean to others, you realize you have power to inspire and transmit courage, and you choose, in every interaction, every day, to connect to your own purpose on the planet.

Articulate Well the Vision and Strategies of the Organization

In organizations, "vision" refers to a clear expression of the future it seeks to create to realize its essential purpose. As a piece of a larger framework that includes the organizational mission and underlying values (Senge, 1990), shared visions are powerful tools for establishing resonance throughout organizations. Leaders who wish to increase their ability to respond to adversity with resilience, therefore, mindfully employ the vision of the organization to create a high level of resonance.

In *Resonant Leadership,* Boyatzis and McKee (2005) emphasize the point that the organizational vision must be shared and it must be inspirational; it must express a better future that drives people to action. Writing in the *Fifth Discipline* about how the vision inspires people to action, Peter Senge describes how visions begin to create resonance. He writes, "Visions spread because of a reinforcing process of increasing clarity, enthusiasm, communication and commitment. As people talk, the vision grows clearer. As it gets clearer, enthusiasm for its benefits build" (p. 227). Moreover, the leader must understand the vision inside and out. Boyatzis and McKee write, "You cannot inspire others about a vision if you yourself cannot articulate it" (p. 164).

When it comes to keeping people focused and pulling in the same direction, resilient leaders doggedly bring every conversation back to the organizational vision. According to Superintendent Rick Miller, championing the shared organizational vision is an act of leadership. Miller says, "Leaders cast a vision developed on the best of what we know to achieve the mission for their community, and then they develop consensus around it. Once people are committed to the shared vision, the leader must be a continual advocate and cheerleader for it." Superintendent Bob Dubick adds, "You have to share your vision with as many people as you can, including community leaders who may or may not have an impact. You never know when something you say will connect and spark support."

Leaders who consistently and publicly champion the shared vision of the organization touch the large number of stakeholders who presumably had a hand and a voice in shaping it. The ability of the organization's vision to reach deep into the passion of so many stakeholders is one reason why it is a powerful tool for creating and sustaining resonance throughout the organization. Superintendent Mark Bielang says, "When you keep the vision front and center you remind people that they want something more. Especially when we have to make tough decisions the vision helps us stay focused so we can make tough decisions that are also good decisions. The vision helps people move forward in developing ideas."

Have a Sense of Humor

Often, the hard lessons in life contain the seeds of mirth—even if only in hindsight. I think back to a time when I was assistant principal in a middle school and believed I witnessed a student do something wildly inappropriate with the hot dog bun served with his cafeteria lunch. After I hauled him into the office and called his father, a group of kids who were not necessarily friends of the accused, came to my office en masse to testify in no uncertain terms that I was wrong. This event, forever known as "The Hot Dog Incident," burned for a while, but it taught me one of the most important principles in student discipline: First, conduct an unbiased investigation. Eventually, of course, this story provided endless opportunities for hilarity within the leadership team as we recounted it (and as some embellished it) over and over again.

A sense of humor not only unites people and creates resonance in the environment, but it can lend a healthier perspective to disruptive events from the outset. As Superintendent Bettye Ray wisely says (and as my hot dog incident proves), "We make mistakes if we get too serious about anything." California superintendent Dale Marsden agrees. He says, "Don't take yourself so seriously that you forget why you are here. I'm not talking about making light of serious situations; I'm talking about not taking *yourself* so seriously. Remember, you are here to do work you love."

Having a sense of humor, especially when it is self-directed and done appropriately, makes you stronger and more resilient. Superintendent Marilyn Birnbaum says, "Humor about yourself helps you develop a thicker skin. The first time you can laugh at yourself you feel a little sting. By the time you are able to laugh at yourself the tenth time, you see that it isn't so painful. This sets a great example for others too—especially when you emphasize the lesson learned from whatever happened. Superintendent Mark Bielang agrees. He says, "A thicker skin comes from injuries." Birnbaum adds, "If we didn't have a sense of humor, we wouldn't survive."

Take Care of Yourself

Leaders who become dissonant are usually in desperate need of renewal. They have neglected their own health and emotional needs in favor of their work and it shows: They are pessimistic, tired, cranky, impatient, and fragile. These leaders make more mistakes and poorer decisions. They alienate people and undermine relationships, which in turn undermines their leadership resilience.

Even when work is meaningful, leaders who respond to constant streams of stress by working harder and giving more ultimately experience distress and may even burn themselves out. Boyatzis and McKee call this pattern of stress without renewal "the syndrome of sacrifice, stress and dissonance" (p. 7). When leaders become dissonant, they contribute to unhealthy stress within the organization, which only compounds their troubles and continues and deepens the syndrome.

The way out of dissonance is through renewal, which is the subject of the next chapter.

SUMMARY

Whether you are a veteran leader or a novice leader, striving toward resonance will make you more resilient. Leaders become more resilient by asking thoughtful leadership questions and through listening to people talk about their experience while remaining aware of and regulating their own emotions—by not letting their buttons get pushed. At the same time, these leaders focus on broadcasting a compelling vision of the future, often referring to the emotional investment of themselves and others in the vision. Resonant leaders develop an awareness of how they inspire—or don't inspire—others, and they take steps to cultivate emotional styles that move people to action.

ACTIVITIES AND QUESTIONS FOR STUDY GROUPS AND TEAMS

1. Recall an occasion when you were keenly aware that your emotional state of being was being corrupted by someone else's dissonance.

   a. What do you remember feeling and thinking?
      - I remember feeling these emotions:
      - I remember thinking these thoughts:
   b. What happened next—were you able to pull yourself out of spiraling into dissonance, or did you lose your balance and equanimity?
   c. Either way, what were your interactions with others like immediately afterward?
   d. How did *you feel* after those interactions?

2. Pay attention to the first inkling of a destructive emotion (anger, fear, attachment) and stare back at it (recognize it for what it is and redirect your thoughts).

3. When you are in a difficult or unpleasant situation, do you maintain your presence, or do you either disengage and shut down or become overly aggressive for the situation?

4. What emotional tone do you add to meetings or gatherings? How would others answer this question about you?

5. What makes you dissonant? What impact does it have on others when you are fearful, angry, or without hope or faith?

6. What does it take for you to pull yourself out of a dissonant funk? Once you decide to become more resonant, how long does it take you to do so?

7. How do you know when you are headed toward a dissonant state of mind? What patterns are present in the hours preceding this?

8. Who do you know who is really great to be with? Why exactly is that? What does this person do? What does he or she say? What does his or her presence do for you? Do you think differently or feel differently around this person?

9. What emotions describe your family, organization, or work team? How many would you say are positive, such as *happy, optimistic, excited, creative, kind,* and *generous?* How many would you say are negative, such as *fearful, depressed, lonely, secretive, jealous,* or *miserly?*

10. Who in your life would benefit from a compassionate perspective? Who empathizes with you but also has constructive input for you to think about? Who needs your compassionate perspective?

11. Pick an important innovation or strategy in your organization and list the goals it is designed to improve. List the incremental wins that have brought you closer to the goal. Remember, small wins are anything more of what you want to see—even in big goals that you are far from completing.

12. Brainstorm ways to commemorate small and early wins that involve the people doing the work and the people whose lives are made better as a result of the work. Let them tell stories about how things are going and the positive changes that have occurred.

13. Stop talking about your circle of control (I suspect "control" is an illusion) and start talking about your circle of influence.

5 Renewal

This is your world. Shape it, or someone else will.

—Gary Lew

Personal renewal is essential to leadership resilience. After all, if you lack the energy to *show up strong* for the demands of leadership, how can you lead forward in times of change? Without renewal, how can you creatively respond to the windfalls and silver linings hidden in adversity? When you are tired and demoralized, how do you think optimistically and creatively? When disruptive change occurs and you need to lead people forward into new realities, you will draw on the energy that comes from the resilience enabler of Renewal. As with the other two resilience enablers, renewal must be cultivated every day; you cannot wait for adversity to hit before you engage in renewal.

A RENEWAL INVENTORY

Before reading on, take a few moments to respond to the Renewal Inventory (to take the online version, visit www.WisdomOut.com) depicted in Exercise 5.1, which will provide you with objective feedback about your current state of renewal. If you are reading this book as a leadership team, replace "I" with "We."

Instructions: Respond to the statements in Exercise 5.1 quickly, providing your first impulse as the answer. If you are responding as a team, look at the average response or look at the amount of responses for each number in the range. A response of 10 is the strongest possible agreement, and 1 is the strongest possible disagreement. There are no correct answers.

Exercise 5.1   The Renewal Inventory

Statement	Strongly Disagree								Strongly Agree	
1. Even if I'm meeting my usual goals and being very efficient on my job, I'm not completely fulfilled unless I am achieving a higher purpose serving the greater good.	1	2	3	4	5	6	7	8	9	10
2. I can think of several times when, after experiencing adversity, I ultimately feel I am better off.	1	2	3	4	5	6	7	8	9	10
3. I can identify very specifically the source of my greatest inspiration.	1	2	3	4	5	6	7	8	9	10
4. When I need physical renewal, I know of specific and consistent activities and routines that will be helpful for me.	1	2	3	4	5	6	7	8	9	10
5. I am very aware of when I need renewal and I know the warning signs that suggest to me that I need support and renewal.	1	2	3	4	5	6	7	8	9	10
6. I am able to reflect on my past and think about mistakes I have made without being obsessed and overwhelmed by them. I know my "lessons learned" and can apply them to my daily life.	1	2	3	4	5	6	7	8	9	10

Statement	Strongly Disagree								Strongly Agree	
7. I have forgiven myself for my past mistakes.	1	2	3	4	5	6	7	8	9	10
8. When I need emotional renewal, I know of people and practices that help me restore my emotional energy.	1	2	3	4	5	6	7	8	9	10
9. I have forgiven others, even those who have hurt me very deeply.	1	2	3	4	5	6	7	8	9	10
10. I can think of a specific example when I have helped to provide renewal to a colleague or a loved one within the past week.	1	2	3	4	5	6	7	8	9	10

Total score: _____

Interpreting Your Score

Where do highly resilient leaders tend to score on the Renewal Inventory? Leaders who take the online version of the Renewal Inventory, and who also rate themselves high on happiness and meaningful work, score most often in the range of 71–100.

If You Score in the Range of 10–40: You are so emotionally and physically exhausted it's amazing that you have the energy to read this book. The physical, emotional, and mental challenges you face all run together, and the effects may be showing up in your sleep and eating habits. Even a walk around the block can feel like an insurmountable challenge to you. Most of all, you are very alone. You can be in a crowd in Times Square, among family and friends who care about you, or lying on your couch into the 10th hour of a television and ice cream marathon—it doesn't matter. It's all the same feeling of isolation and despair. You need a break—in every sense of the word—and the sooner you make the break from this landscape of disease, the sooner you will begin the road to renewal.

If You Score in the Range of 41–70: In a nutshell, although you may know how to renew, you may have difficulty taking action. Although you occasionally find new energy, it sometimes feels as if you are treading water in the middle of a vast ocean and there isn't much for you to hang on to when the waves crash around you. Perhaps the most disconcerting statement that others make when they refer to your successes at work or your apparently happy personal life is that "you've got it all." But there are days when the successes on which other people focus offer little or no fulfillment to you. Promotions and raises come and go, and you accept congratulations with little real enthusiasm. When your friends and colleagues express envy of you, you are thinking, "If you only knew how little this means to me." There are exceptions, of course, as you consider moments of physical, emotional, and mental renewal in the past. You sometimes think about recreating those moments, but transforming thought into action is inconsistent and distant.

If You Score in the Range of 71–100: You have found the sources of renewal in your life and you regularly use them, and this gives you the energy you need to "show up for your life." Although you can certainly be effective in your professional life and you are capable of maintaining and sustaining meaningful personal relationships, you find true meaning in service and a contribution to the greater good. You are not superhuman, but you seem to have a level of calm and equanimity that allows you to keep your cool when other people around you panic. You have faced disappointment and loss, and you endure not through blind stoicism but through renewal. When your body and spirit are down, you show the wisdom to stop, rest, and restore yourself, meeting your mental, physical, and spiritual needs. As successful as you are, you are the first to acknowledge that you have not achieved this success alone. You are regularly aware of the role that other people—today and in history—have played in your success. Although you rarely claim credit for it, your personal example serves as sources of renewal for other people.

Reflection

Take a moment to reflect on the results of your Renewal Inventory.

My Renewal Inventory Score is: _____

Highlight key insights from the score interpretation you received. What sounds "right" to you? What seems off? What goals do you want to set for yourself or for your team?

_____

_____

_____

_____

_____

_____

HOW RENEWAL ENABLES LEADERSHIP RESILIENCE

If you were to read this paragraph while holding your breath, in a matter of seconds you would be acutely aware of the urge to breathe. The uncomfortable sensation you will feel, known as "air hunger," is triggered not as you might expect by a lack of oxygen, but by high levels of carbon dioxide accumulating in your blood. Ordinarily you do not need to think about breathing. Unsolicited by your conscious mind, the respiratory control center located in your brain stem monitors your carbon dioxide levels, and when they are out of whack, orders your breathing muscles to take in air. Lucky for all of us, normal breathing is an automated function of the human body.

Though more subtle (and therefore, significantly more dangerous), the absence of renewal in leadership also creates a sensation of need, experienced as vague feelings of edginess, restlessness, and the sense that life just is not all that it could be. Unfortunately, many leaders ignore these signals, and because it can take years before their accumulated effects take a toll (often dramatically in the form of heart disease, car accidents, addictions, depression, or divorce), they do not take steps to build in a regular practice of renewal. Some leaders even go so far as to *expect* to suffer from the demands of leadership. They believe that giving up exercise, play, sleep, relaxation, and family is fair collateral for doing the work they have chosen to do. Leaders who buy into this narrative fail to see the connection between renewal and the ability to lead with stamina, creativity, and joy—qualities that signal resilience.

In his book *Predictably Irrational: The Hidden Forces That Shape Our Destiny* (2010), behavioral economist Dan Airely writes about the research of Ralph Keeney, including the alarming information that premature deaths of people aged 15–64 have increased from 5% in 1900 to 55% in 2000—mostly due to poor personal choices such as overeating, smoking, unsafe sex, sedentary lifestyle, and driving without a seatbelt. Airely adds the estimation that "about half of us will make a lifestyle decision that will lead us to an early grave" (p. 166). A persistent lack of renewal does more than diminish your health and lifespan, however. In organizations, a lack of renewal puts people on a path toward "burnout," which according to the 2007–2008 Towers Perrin Survey of nearly 90,000 employees worldwide is the leading cause of employee disengagement—a condition that most certainly undermines leadership resilience.

RENEWAL, CREATIVITY, AND PROBLEM SOLVING

Personal renewal is important for your health and well-being—it allows you to show up for your life, and it gives you energy to do meaningful work.

But doing things that make you feel good and give you energy can also make you think better. Renewal provides you with the interludes you need to solve complex problems with creativity.

For example, I'm one of those people who think better when I am moving. While in my home office, I do at least 50% of my work while walking on a treadmill desk. I also use a web-based gizmo called Fitbit that records the number of steps and stairs I take each day and connects to a website where I can keep track of the food I eat. But when it comes to personal renewal, running is my fondest activity. I'm not a fast runner; my marathon motto is "start slow and taper off," but I can run long and far. While running, I have the most amazing insights about the dilemmas currently facing me. Before I learned how to use the recording app on my iPhone, I would forget most of these great ideas by the time I ran home and could write them down. Now that I'm better at working my smartphone, I have sent myself countless endorphin-bathed messages containing crystal-clear thoughts about my life and work. I confess: not all of the insights sustain their brilliance when I lose my runner's high. But some actually prove quite useful and, for good or ill, many have made their way into this book.

Interludes of Renewal

If your natural tendency is to adopt a workaholic approach to life, not only are you jeopardizing your health, but you might actually be preventing the breakthrough thinking you desire and need. Consider that a 2009 study from the Center for Creative Leadership finds that many high-flying founders and executives also engage in regular physical exercise. For these leaders, taking time off to hit the gym contributed to their success. Other leaders gain the same kind of energy from cooking, gardening, seeing all the Sundance Film Festival films, rescuing greyhound dogs, or dressing up as Brad Majors, the hero from *The Rocky Horror Picture Show* and attending weekly midnight screenings. No matter what personal renewal you decide to take part in, the most important thing is that you use the resulting energy to "show up" for your life and take advantage of all of the opportunities and challenges that life brings. The trick is to have the discipline to leave the task at hand when your mind is stuck, and engage in interludes of renewal.

For former superintendent Carmella Franco, renewal comes in quiet contemplation at the end of the day, often in the garden or walking alone. Franco says, "When I feel the heavy thoughts of the day come down on me, I simply make up my mind not to ruminate on the negative. Instead I move on to more solution-oriented thoughts. I jot a few words down and leave them out where I can see them. Then, as I garden or walk or just sit quietly and relax, the answer comes to me." When the best answer comes to Franco it often feels like a "eureka!" moment. She told me, "When the answer comes and it feels right, I know it holds the insight I need."

The journey toward inspired thought often ends in a simple sense of joy and delight. The process is complex, however, beginning with two preconditions in the brain: (1) the presence of connected neural networks of information and (2) the ability those networks have to adapt, to form and reform into new and novel connections (Johnson, 2010). In his recent book, *The Brain and Emotional Intelligence: New Insights,* Daniel Goleman (2011) emphasizes the role of neural networks during creative thought, and their ability to adapt and connect. He says that EEGs of people during a creative moment show that the instant before answers come, the brain spikes with Gamma activity (this spike, by the way, is what creates that little thrill you experience when you have an "a-ha!" moment). Goleman writes, "Gamma activity indicates the binding together of neurons, as far-flung brain cells connect in a new neural network—as when a new association emerges. Immediately after that gamma spike, the new idea enters our consciousness" (Kindle Location 223).

INSPIRED THOUGHT FOR TEAMS

When making decisions, many leaders and their teams traverse through a phase of brainstorming—which is an ideal stage for inspired thought. To leverage inspired thought while making important team decisions, follow these steps during the brainstorming phase:

1. After discussing the decision that needs to be made, divide the group into small groups of about three people each. The groups go for a 15- to 30-minute walk together. As the groups walk, they focus on the issue at hand (without digressions) and they brainstorm solutions. Record the ideas that emerge on a smartphone.

2. The whole group reassembles and shares the results of the brainstorm.

3. Facilitate a process of advocacy and inquiry (Senge, 1990) to understand each idea fully. Invite walking partners to talk about their favorite ideas and explain the merits (advocacy) as they see them, of each. After a period of advocacy, switch to inquiry. Invite others to ask questions and uncover faulty assumptions.

4. As a group, go do something else together in the community. Visit a museum, an art gallery, or take a tour of the local fire department or local university campus. Explore and let your minds wander and wonder. (Fear not, your subliminal thoughts will simultaneously focus on the issues facing the team.)

5. Come back together and make the decision.

6. E-mail me at elle@wisdomout.com or call me at 925-786-0987 and tell me what happened. (Be prepared for me to invite you to "guest star" on a webinar so you can share your story with other leaders!)

Learn and Explore

Translated into practical action, the preconditions in the brain for inspired thought imply that you must be a voracious learner and an adventurous experiencer of life. You have to go where what you know in your specialty area has a chance to bump up against ideas in fields other than your own; you have to live big (which may explain why most resilient leaders love the challenge of working for a greater good—it forces them into bigger risks and bigger experiences). In the classic book, *A Whack on the Side of the Head: How You Can Be More Creative*, Roger von Oech encourages those in search of creative problem solving to become explorers. Quoting journalist Robert Wieder, von Oech writes, "Anyone can look for fashion in a boutique or history in a museum. The creative person looks for history in a hardware store and fashion in an airport" (p. 108).

School leaders who lack the "explorer" perspective are often in the habit of canceling special events in order to put out fires or stay in the office to do more work. They deprive themselves of the very life experiences that lead to inspired thought and action. At a recent evening event, for example, California superintendent Robert Haley looked around the room and, noticing several empty seats, commented on how difficult it is for school leaders to choose to detach from the challenges of the day. Haley said, "I had a hard day and it was tempting not to drive into the city to attend this meeting. But I'm so glad I came. After listening to the great presentations and having the chance to chat with different colleagues, I feel renewed and reenergized. I'm going back to my district with good ideas and new perspectives that help me more clearly see the issues at hand."

Think Better

Steven Johnson, author of the book *Where Good Ideas Come From: The Natural History of Innovation* (2010), tells the story of Stephane Tarnier, an obstetrician living in Paris in the late 1870s. One day, Dr. Tarnier took a day off from work to go to the zoo. Lingering at an exhibit of newly hatched chicks, tumbling about inside a heated box, Dr. Tarnier suddenly saw how the same concept could also work for human newborns. In no time at all, the good doctor hired the zoo poultry raiser to build a similar device for the hospital. Once installed and in use, Dr. Tarnier went on to conduct crucial research to prove that the incubator could save the lives of ailing and premature infants. Thank goodness Dr. Tarnier took a day off to go to the zoo!

Children seem to instinctively know that interludes of renewal make you think better. At The Tinkering School located in California, for example, kids gather for two weeks at a time to invent stuff. They are given access to raw supplies and tools, and work with a team to invent something mechanical. In a 2009 TED talk, Gever Tulley, camp founder and director, said he notices that the kids do something rather amazing when they run into a quandary with their inventions: they get down on their bellies and they decorate them. Tulley said, "It is here, in these interludes, that the kids have the breakthrough thoughts. The interludes provide periods of time for conceptual incubation."

The stories of Dr. Tarnier and other leaders provide evidence that renewal does more than create energy to get through the day. It also provides room for inspired thought, *especially* needed during times of adversity when yesterday's solutions fall short in new realities. Taking a cue from children, your road to renewal might also come from play or stimulations associated with the right brain (Pink, 2009), indulged in after hours, on weekends, and on vacations where you escape from your usual routines. Travel, arts and crafts, metaphor, performing arts, music, tours of exhibits, playing with the dog, hiking, cooking, poetry, photography, storytelling—all of these are portals to renewal.

If you still doubt that renewal is key to breakthrough thinking, test it yourself by noticing when inspired thought strikes you and what others tell you about when good ideas come to them. For example, I just love the e-mail sent to me by one of my colleagues about a tricky data analysis project we were working on together. Her e-mail said, "I had an insight last night in the hot tub, to look at a couple of cohort groups." It turned out her "hot tub idea" was a good one; when she drilled into the data, she discovered a positive trend in reading for two groups of students—data that provided hope and focus to a high school faculty that previously had neither.

While renewal does not eliminate the demands of life and work, it does provide energy for individuals, teams, and systems to remain creative and relevant while meeting those demands. Renewal creates interludes; time where your brain can literally go "right" (instead of spinning in left brain) and think more creatively—even about complex problems.

ON-THE-JOB RENEWAL

Just as engaging in your favorite activities outside the workday is critical to inspired thought, on-the-job interludes of renewal help you sustain your energy and ability to think creatively throughout the workday.

Given the importance of renewal to personal energy and innovation, I find it important and exciting to understand what organizations can do to promote and support renewal on the job. For years, I have been writing about on-the-job happiness as a source of energy and renewal for leaders who are passionately engaged in meaningful work (Allison et al., 2012). In 2011, I began asking leaders to tell me what gives them happiness and energy on the job and during the workday. In this ongoing study, responses from leaders have rendered hundreds of data points that provide clues about the characteristics of systems that promote energy in people (to participate, please visit www.WisdomOut.com and select "Participate" and "The Happiness Research" from the menu).

What might surprise and please you to learn is that what leaders find most energizing on the job has very little to do with taking breaks, surfing the Internet, gossiping, and otherwise escaping the demands of the organization, and more to do with experiencing relationships, problem solving, learning, and making a difference for stakeholders.

Sources of Workplace Energy and Joy

Figure 5.1 displays the on-the-job energy sources named by leaders most often when I asked for their top three.

As you can see, the leaders in this study report an increase in energy when they focus on meaningful work and meaningful relationships. Not surprising, given most educational leaders' penchant for learning, many of the same sources of on-the-job energy also describe job-embedded professional development (Brown-Easton, 2008) and learning organizations (Senge, 1990).

Figure 5.1   Sources of On-the-Job Energy and Joy

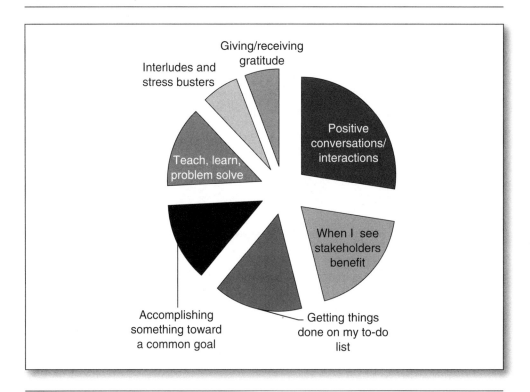

Charlotte Fritz, who is an assistant professor in organizational psychology at Portland State University, also conducted research and discovered results related to mine. In an interview with Fritz that appeared in the May 2012 *Harvard Business Review* she says, "Taking short breaks during the workday doesn't revitalize you—unless you do something job related and positive such as praising a colleague or learning something new" (p. 34).

Based on the results of my research about what brings people on-the-job joy and energy, combined with the prevailing assumption that workday focus is a source of renewal for resilient leadership, I offer you several examples of on-the-job interludes (Allison, 2011). What will you add to this list?

Ideas for On-the-Job Interludes That Also Sustain Your Focus on Work

1. **Lunch and Listen Part 1.** Eat lunch with someone who will just listen (not give advice or tell you what to do) as you describe something you love about your work. Limit lunch to one hour. Stay focused; no gossip.

2. **Lunch and Listen Part 2.** Take an aspiring leader to lunch with the specific intent to listen, just listen to *them* (not give advice or tell them what to do) as they describe what they think is possible in their work. Limit lunch to one hour. Stay focused; no gossip.

3. **Find the Stories.** Interview stakeholders, colleagues, and students about something your organization did for them. Take digital photos of each person and put them in a scrapbook along with a couple of quotes from the conversation. Later, when you need renewal and inspiration, thumb through the scrapbook and be reminded about how your work makes a difference. After you make the scrapbook, upload the photos into a digital photo frame where they constantly scroll and infuse the workplace with positive energy.

4. **Walk and Learn.** Walk down the hall and ask one or two people to tell you what they've learned today. Be sure to tell them that the reason you are asking this question is so *you* can feel renewed. This will make people more forthcoming because they want to be of support to you.

5. **My Favorite Mistake.** Make a 10-minute renewal date with someone you work with. When you meet up, tell your coworker about your "favorite mistake"—something related to your meaningful work that might have gone wrong, but that taught you the most valuable lesson.

6. **See Systemic Connections.** Make a list of the decisions facing you over the next 12 months. Then make another list of the data you'll look at (including surveys, focus groups, trend data, quarterly data) needed for each decision. Notice the overlap and do a happy dance about that. You see, complex decisions usually have systemic connections, so you can leverage information that helps with one decision, to another decision.

7. **Get Some Coaching.** Schedule a coaching session with someone you work with who has great coaching skills and will ask you the kind of thought leadership questions that create breakthroughs in your thinking. Send them a thank-you card afterward with an invitation to reciprocate. Senior leaders who coach their colleagues and direct reports learn more about the work of others and gain insight into the whole system.

8. **Thanks for the Opportunity.** Write a thank-you note to someone for something they allowed you to do to make the organization better. Deliver it to them in person if you can. They may be perplexed at first, "Say what? You're thanking me for something you did?" Tell them you are thanking them because they gave you the chance to lead and grow.

9. **Thanks in Advance.** Write a thank-you-in-advance note to someone expressing your gratitude in advance for something you need from them. You'll learn how to ask for what you need, and you'll experience gratitude, which is a source of renewal and energy. The other person gains the experience of giving and supporting a colleague.

10. **Have a Research Date.** Pick up one of your "go to" professional journals that you never get to read and skim the table of contents, looking for something that sparks your curiosity. Make one copy of the article, bring it to a colleague, and ask him or her to meet you for lunch or a break where you can read it together and talk about it. Your colleague gets to pick the article the next time.

11. **Make an Artistic Display of Data.** Review key indicators for a project you are leading. Get a poster sheet and markers and represent the data in a format you've never considered before. Or, go to a website such as www.easel.ly that allows you to make infographics for free. Explain your data display with your team.

If you try some of these ideas out, I'd love to hear how they worked for you. Send me an e-mail at elle@wisdomout.com.

When your brief on-the-job interludes sustain your focus on work, you accomplish more during the workday. This, combined with longer episodes of renewal and rejuvenation outside of the workday—going to the zoo, taking vacations, not working on most weekends—create positive conditions for resilient leadership; not only will you have more energy to accomplish meaningful work, but you will experience greater creativity that leads to insight *and* you will accomplish more during the workday—which gives you more time off for renewal outside of work. Talk about a win-win-win proposition.

CULTIVATING RENEWAL TO ENABLE RESILIENCE

Leaders who engage in renewal outside of work and in short interludes during the workday increase their leadership resilience. Not only do they enjoy enhanced physical and emotional health, but they also increase their ability to manage their emotions, think well, and meet the demands of the day. Difficult though it may be, resilient leaders choose to make lifestyle choices that promote their health and prolong their lives. These choices not only make you a more resilient leader, but they also enhance your well-being and they simply make life more delightful and work more satisfying.

The Greater Good: The Deepest Well

Hands down, the deepest well of renewal for resilient leaders comes from doing work that matters—work for a greater good. Reciprocally, meaningful work inspires resilient leaders to take good care of themselves, which enables them to accomplish even *more* meaningful work. The greater good gives meaning to the struggle. Superintendent Bob Dubick puts it best. He says, "I get energy from doing good work, from making a difference for families. For me renewal comes from knowing that I make a difference and that I'm doing the right things. Knowing that I do the right things gives me strength to show up every day and do more right things."

Superintendent Patty Wool remembers the challenge she faced early in her tenure as principal of a high-performing middle school where, justified by their record of success up to this point, the veteran staff resisted professional development. A few vocal faculty members, who persuaded others to agree with them, believed they already were the "experts" who clearly knew what they needed to sustain their success. But Wool knew that even high-performing schools do not remain so if the faculty is not continually questioning and learning. Considering the peccadillos and needs of the faculty, but not willing to ignore professional development and primarily, the changing needs of the students, Wool proposed they learn the process of action research and then work together in interdisciplinary teams to investigate research questions about their practice. Because of the unique way it places teachers at the center of their own learning, action research turned out to resonate with Wool's veteran faculty. Wool told me, "After a year of resistance and pushback to professional development, we found a fit in action research." Wool's story has a great coda: through action research the faculty also learned coaching and collaboration—two other skills they had resisted up to this point. Wool told me, "When I look back on this experience I realize that it was so important for me to make a difference for students, yet do it in a way that would create a real difference and have a lasting impact. This is what makes me resilient."

What Makes a Greater Good?

The greater good is not an abstract principle even if at first it may be challenging to apprehend. Put simply, the greater good is a conscious creation of results that produce benefits that transcend the needs of any one person or group to benefit more people and groups, especially the most vulnerable, and for the long term (Allison et al., 2012).

Here is an example of the greater good in action that most educational leaders can relate to: While average educational leaders seek to satisfy the basic requirements of adequate yearly progress goals and minimal standards (and even try to mathematically calculate who is "close to achieving" and then help only those students), leaders who are motivated by a greater good seek to exceed standards for all students *and* change the conditions that allowed achievement gaps to grow and persist in the first place. Michael Fullan (1993) puts it this way: "Education has a moral purpose . . . to make a difference in the lives of students regardless of background, and to help produce citizens who can live and work productively in increasingly dynamic complex societies" (p. 4).

Most educators find that the qualities that signal a greater good are also rewarding in their own right. They stimulate emotions of compassion and gratitude, both of which are known to elicit a sense of well-being. How would producing the following qualities of the greater good also bring renewal to you?

- The greater good is inclusive: It seeks to create benefits for all students—the high achievers *and* the most vulnerable whose success is in jeopardy.
- The greater good seeks to create important, needed, and meaningful change in order to benefit many people and the surrounding context.
- The greater good is a by-product of many people tackling complex, persistent, and vexing problems from different angles.
- The greater good seeks insight from problems rather than just contain them.

- The greater good considers the impact on future generations for the long term and builds in safeguards to minimize unintentional consequences.
- The greater good is made visible through action taken by those who see the need for change.
- The greater good is brought about by individuals seeking real accomplishment and humbly accepting accolades as by-products of meaningful work.
- The greater good arises out of processes that align with the outcomes; the end does not justify the means.
- The greater good is coherent to the mission and highest purpose of the organization.
- The greater good creates and opens up leadership opportunities for others.
- The greater good simultaneously transforms the culture surrounding the initiative in order to create partnerships that empower people to renew and therefore sustain the initiative.
- The greater good is often fueled by personal passion that begs to manifest through the leader's role.

Consider the Greater Good in All You Do

When you begin new projects or revitalize existing projects, you can top off your resilience-enabling powers by mindfully building in consideration for the greater good. In *Flywheel: Transformational Leadership Coaching for Sustainable Change* (2013), my book on leadership coaching, I devote an entire chapter to the topic of the greater good and provide the tool you see in Exercise 5.2 to help leaders more consciously design meaningful work that promotes renewal. As with all of the tools in this book, you can use it for your individual work or for collaborative work with your teams.

Deal With Busyness

At this point, you might be thinking, *"All this talk of the greater good is well and fine, Elle, but we're already working hard and people are exhausted and stressed out. We're just too busy to do anything more."* Webster's New World Dictionary defines busy as "used up, not available, as with a telephone." Not a glamorous definition of leadership by anyone's terms, yet many leaders spend inordinate amounts of time telling others just how busy they are. An unrelenting sense of "busyness" is a sure signal that you are spending more time putting out fires and being distracted by short-term tasks, and less time engaged in meaningful work. As if all that were not bad enough, busyness is also one of the most pervasive sources of stress.

Exercise 5.2 A Process to Vet Projects for a Greater Good

Instructions: Use the worksheet below to help the leaders you coach select their coaching projects.

Step 1. First list titles for the top five meaningful work projects that you lead or could lead, given your position in the organization and your personal passions. These projects could already be on your plate or they could be projects you need to start or revive, or they could be something you have been longing to do because you know they would be good for people and for the organization. These projects might advance new initiatives or they might refine, revise, or deepen existing initiatives.

Title your top five project possibilities and list them here:

Project Possibility 1: _____

Project Possibility 2: _____

Project Possibility 3: _____

Project Possibility 4: _____

Project Possibility 5: _____

Step 2. Now, copy the table below for each project possibility you listed above and write the project title on the top line. With that project in mind, assign a number (1–5), with 1 indicating the lowest presence of the quality and 5 indicating the highest amount of the quality, for each item.

Vetting Process

Project Possibility Title: _____

Project Qualities for a Greater Good. The extent to which this project:							
1. Is something I feel personally passionate about and can begin now.	2. Aligns with and is coherent with the goals of the organization and serves to advance the mission.	3. Builds leadership in others and gives them opportunities to lead.	4. Seeks to create solutions to vexing problems in my organization and/or the greater field of education.	5. Mobilizes the best of what we know about great teaching, learning, and leadership.	6. Is something I can lead through the influence and work of my role and reputation.	7. Will ultimately create benefits for all students and stakeholders, especially those who are most vulnerable.	
1–5	**1–5**	**1–5**	**1–5**	**1–5**	**1–5**	**1–5**	**TOTAL SCORE**
Your Score:	Your Score:	Your Score:	Your Score:	Your Score:	Your Score:	Your Score:	
Notes and Reflection:	Notes and Reflection:	Notes and Reflection:	Notes and Reflection:	Notes and Reflection:	Notes and Reflection:	Notes and Reflection:	

The Price of Busyness

Busyness often signals a lack of focus. Leaders who lose their battle with busyness are so overwhelmed with daily demands and putting out fires that they do not have energy, let alone time, for aspirational work. What to do about busyness? Ironically, there is nothing like a new and *meaningful* project to cure a leader of busyness and focus their time and energy. Although it will feel counterintuitive to busy leaders, you do yourself a service when you get going on a complex project that matters to you and that serves your organization. When you do, you will have no other choice but to reprioritize less important obligations and needs.

Play a Bigger Game

If you used the greater good vetting tool (brought up earlier in this chapter), and your work or the work of your team came up short, you may become aware that you are leading small—doing good work perhaps, but not stepping up to have a wider, deeper, more sustainable impact on people and the system. Sure, your mistakes might be fewer and of less consequence but there is little reward in making small mistakes because you lead small.

When you play a bigger game, important leadership projects become even more compelling, more inspiring, and therefore, more sustainable and busyness takes a back seat. The ideas presented in the following box are entry points for you to "up the ante" and play a bigger game.

WAYS TO "UP THE ANTE," PLAY A BIGGER GAME, AND THEREBY EDGE OUT BUSYNESS

- Open your classroom to demonstrate effective practices for novice teachers, or invite a novice administrator to shadow you for a day or more.
- Write and speak about your work in order to contribute to the knowledge of others in the field (new perspectives, new applications of common perspectives, ideas that may be contrary to conventional wisdom, new tools).
- Take an effective initiative already in place to a deeper level of implementation.
- Reengineer a cumbersome process so people can achieve results more efficiently and with less stress.
- Build partnerships where none currently exist.
- Apply knowledge and skills to a new problem or in a new way.
- Make explicit the cohesion your work has to other work in the organization.

(Continued)

(Continued)

- Ask others to take leadership roles within the projects you lead.
- Add a teaching/mentoring/professional development component to an initiative or project you lead.
- Make sure benefits from initiatives flow to the most vulnerable stakeholders.
- Remove barriers and revise unhelpful policies.
- Apply an existing service, product, or process to create social justice.
- Collect stories to add to disaggregated data in order to build a full profile of information.
- Involve others in early experimentation, testing, and revision of a new initiative.
- Extend an existing initiative to include a new group of students, teachers, or administrators.

Manage Your Stress: A Dreadful Robber of Energy and Happiness

Like "air hunger" in the context of leadership, the need for renewal comes not so much from a lack of free time, coffee breaks, and vacations, as it does from the *presence* of multiple, myriad stresses that threaten to overwhelm us. Renewal, in all of its various forms, is the antidote to leadership stress. While engaging in meaningful work may be the greatest source of renewal for resilient educational leaders, unmanaged and unrelenting stress efficiently undermines it. New understandings about the science behind stress strongly recommend that renewal for stress reduction become a priority in all of our lives.

Telomeres

To get the conversation started, let me introduce you to the miraculous placement of telomeres in your cells. First a definition: Telomeres are stubs of DNA that protect the ends of your chromosomes (Epel et al., 2004; de Lange, Lundblad, & Blackburn, 2006). I picture telomeres as duct tape, wrapped around the frayed ends of electrical cords. Blackburn (2009) likens them to aglets, the plastic caps found on the tips of a good pair of shoelaces. Whichever metaphor works for you, you can imagine either one—duct tape or shoelace tips—breaking down over time. In fact, every time your cells replicate, small amounts of your telomeres naturally wear away in the process—just like duct tape and aglets do when they are regularly handled. Eventually the telomeres and the DNA they contain on the chromosomes at the ends of your cells wear away entirely, and the cell naturally dies (Zolli & Healy, 2012). Not to be morbid, but over time, more and more of your cells naturally die. Eventually and inevitably, so do you.

While you seemingly have no control over the natural aging process, you do have some control over stress, which, in addition to normal cell division is another source of wear and tear on telomeres and is an accelerant of the aging process. Here is how stress ages us: During the biological process most of us know as the "fight or flight" response, adrenaline and norepinephrine pumps into your body. This is bad news because it turns out that excess quantities of stress hormones such as adrenaline and norepinephrine also erode your telomeres. To make matters worse, psychological stress can keep you in a steady state of fight or flight, literally bathing your telomeres with potent mixtures of stress hormones that accelerate their degradation (Epel et al., 2004; Goleman, 2011; Sapolsky, 2004).

Now for some good news. An enzyme called telomerase, when present in relevant amounts (which can be detected and measured through blood tests), mitigates the effects of natural aging and stress on your telomeres. And here is the *really* good news: You can increase telomerase in your body by engaging in activities that reduce stress (Blackburn, 2009; Epel et al., 2004; Goleman, 2011; Sapolsky, 2004). You just have to choose to do so.

Ways to Mitigate the Effects of Stress

Writing about the mitigating effects of meditation on stress, Zolli and Healy (2012) quote researchers Jacobs and Saron who conclude, "activities that increase a person's sense of well-being may have a profound effect on the most fundamental aspects of their physiology. It doesn't necessarily have to be meditation per se; it's really about creating conditions in which you can flourish and your purpose can come into being" (p. 140).

Although increased well-being and a corresponding increase in your body's production of telomerase can be achieved in a variety of ways, several strategies come to the forefront for their powerful ability to alleviate stress and increase the lifespan of your telomeres (Epel et al., 2004; Sapolsky, 2004).

- **Physical Exercise.** According to studies conducted by Elizabeth Blackburn at the University of California, San Francisco, exercise is one of the best strategies for mitigating the effects of stress hormones on your telomeres (O'Brien, 2011). If you are not physically active, the best thing you can do for the students and communities you serve is get active now. If you are already active, don't stop, especially when you feel overwhelmed. The impact of a sedentary lifestyle is so pronounced that *Harvard Business Review* blogger Nilofer Merchant (2013) announced, "sitting is the smoking of our generation."
- **Sleep.** New research from the University of California, Berkeley, shows that sleep makes you more than tired and irritable; it also may increase your level of generalized anxiety. Sleep deprivation makes you anxious because it causes other parts of your brain, specifically the amygdala and insular cortex, to go on high alert, producing the

kind of anxiety associated with excessive worrying (Goldstein et al., 2013). When excessive worrying from lack of sleep becomes chronic, it is as if you are in a constant state of fight or flight, a condition that increases stress hormone production.

- **Affinity Groups.** Join a support group or offer to mentor or coach someone else. Researchers Elizabeth Blackburn and Elissa Epel (2009) looked at the benefits of belonging to affinity groups on mothers caring for severely handicapped children and conclude that when it comes to mitigating the deadly effects of stress, belonging to a support group can make a difference—but not primarily for the reason you think. It turns out that belonging to a support group allows you to feel compassion, and the compassion one feels when supporting another person appears to stimulate the production of telomerase. In other words, the compassion you feel when you belong to a group of people who are struggling with issues similar to you also mitigates stress for yourself at a cellular level. Compassion feels good.

- **Reframe Your Perspective.** Every day, large and small stressors challenge even the most optimistic among us. Stress researchers say that when events stress us out, it is often because we feel we have no control over them. True, there are many things in life we cannot control. For everything else, we can choose to reframe the way we look at it (Seligman, 2011a; Singer, 2011).

- **Meditation and Mindfulness Training.** People who are meditation practitioners will tell you that one of the greatest gifts it offers is not learning how to empty one's mind of thought, but of learning to become more *mindful*. Meditation, which is the ability to observe and experience one's thoughts and one's experiences without reacting and without exhibiting emotional upset (Zolli & Healy, 2012), is a powerful antidote to the feelings of disorientation that come with adversity and disruptive change. (See Chapter 6 for a simple exercise to increase mindfulness.)

SUMMARY

In this chapter, we explored the importance of renewal to leadership resilience. Renewal bolsters your leadership resilience; it creates energy for you to "show up" for your life and your work, and it enables you to bounce forward in times of adversity and disruptive change. Renewal helps sustain a healthy mind and body, but it also makes you think better. Interludes of renewal both on the job and off the clock are essential for resilient leadership. Stress and busyness are dreadful robbers of happiness—and therefore, of resilience—and they prevent leaders from getting to meaningful work for the greater good. The good news is that leaders can take steps to mitigate stress and deal with busyness.

ACTIVITIES AND QUESTIONS FOR STUDY GROUPS AND TEAMS

The following list of activities and questions was first published on the Wisdom Out website (Allison-Napolitano, 2011).

1. Exercise! (Feed your telomeres). Watch this YouTube video on telomeres: http://www.youtube.com/watch?v=cvjzwTBjXMI

2. Smile and laugh. Watch this TED talk by Ron Gutman on the hidden power of smiling:

   http://www.ted.com/talks/ron_gutman_the_hidden_power_of_smiling .html

3. To help eliminate a sense of busyness, make a list of 10 things that would take you 15 minutes or less to complete. Before you go to bed each night, do one to three of the items and cross them off your list.

4. Establish a transition activity at the end of the day from work to home. Share your strategy with your colleagues. For example, Superintendent Mike Borgaard's office is about 1 mile from the freeway he takes home. His rule for himself is this: When he hits the freeway, he stops ruminating about work and purposefully thinks about home, family, and his hobbies.

5. Ask for a 20-minute coaching session so you can think through something that matters to the meaningful work you do.

6. Don't sacrifice "good" for the illusion of perfection. (We spend a lot of energy making small things perfect—which is a form of procrastination.)

7. Go to bed 15 minutes earlier.

8. Go for a midday walk.

9. Turn off the "ding" sound on your cell phone and computer.

10. Refuse to use your cell phone when you drive.

11. Mindfully choose to let something urgent but unimportant go. In a short while, it will no longer be urgent and may prove to be irrelevant too. Reflect on the results of this choice.

12. Decide not to say "I'm busy" anymore. Instead, start saying some version of: "I've got a lot on my plate, but it's all good."

Part III

Leadership Resilience in Action

This section illuminates each stage in the nondirectional cycle of Leadership Resilience in Action. Leadership Resilience in Action is a progression of competencies used by leaders as they respond to disruptive change, resistance to change, pushback in the face of change, and the general churn and angst of the organization.

Remember, as you put the cycle into motion, you will draw on the three enabling capacities of Relationships, Resonance, and Renewal.

Introduction to Part III: Leadership Resilience in Action

Apparently, there is nothing that cannot happen today.

—Mark Twain

As was established in Chapter 1, disruptive change is neither unusual nor rare. If you are a leader, stuff happens every day to upset your apple cart. The question is, will you empower yourself and those around you to step confidently into new realities, or will you engender fear and hesitation in the people you lead? The answer to this question depends in part on the quality of the resilience enablers (Relationships, Resonance, and Renewal) presented in the three previous chapters, but it also has much to do with your response to specific events when they happen: your leadership resiliency in action.

The competencies leaders display as they first face and then wrestle with each fresh crisis that comes along builds their reputations. How leaders see things through become the stories people tell when they describe them later, when the dust has settled. This chapter focuses on the cycle of resiliency in action, seen in the top center of the triangle of the Leadership Resilience Model, presented in Chapter 2. The cycle describes the competencies resilient leaders display when disruptions occur, from first learning about the event to reflecting on its resolution. For the cycle to optimally work, leaders must draw on the enabling capacities of Relationships, Resonance, and Renewal, which—if you've been caretaking their existence—are bountiful and accessible.

When facing turmoil and disruptive change, resilient leaders display a cycle of competencies that draw people forward, leverage silver linings, and create positive organizational change. They are:

1. Stay Calm
2. Carry On
3. Accept the New Reality
4. Want Something More
5. Instigate Adaptive Action
6. Reflect & Celebrate

6

Stay Calm

Reminder: As you read this chapter, note where the ideas and strategies presented draw on the leadership resilience-enabling capacities of Relationships, Resonance, and Renewal. Then, at the end of the chapter, write down what you want to learn about or experience in order to bolster the capacities so that you are better able to respond in the aftermath of adversity and disruptive change.

During the first winter I lived in the Iowa countryside, cows licked the paint off my car. How this ridiculous event came to pass makes for a good story. I was driving near my house when I came upon a herd of cows standing stubbornly in the two-lane paved road ahead of me. Previously an urban dweller, I was alarmed. Why weren't these cows in the zoo where they belong?

Concerned for the safety of the bucolic creatures before me, not to the mention the other drivers that might come zooming along, I decided to take action. I flicked on my hazard blinkers, left my car in the middle of the road, and tore up the driveway of the first farm I saw. Reaching the main house, I banged on the front door to roust the farmer within. After what seemed a long time, an older gentleman sporting overalls, a gray crew cut, and an enormous smile that reached the crinkles around his sparkling blue eyes opened the door. Without introduction, I yelled to him my frantic news: Your cows are in the road! I expected to see the farmer grab a coat, throw open the screen door, and race back to the road with me to see to his wayward herd. Instead he held his ground, placed his hands on his hips and roared with laughter. "Well aren't you spunky!" he declared.

In his own good time, Mr. Proskey (who became a terrific friend to me in the months to come) ambled down the drive, commenting on the lovely, crisp winter day. When we reached the road and saw the cows surrounding my car, enormous pink tongues licking away he said, "Uh-oh, looks like they found the salt. Next time, just blow your horn and they'll move along." Next time?

I'm sure the moral of this story is clear to you: Willy-nilly reactions that cause you to run through the streets like Chicken Little usually make matters worse and cause upset for all but the most Zen-like among us. When disruptive change occurs, first do nothing. As it turns out, this is hard enough.

Stay Calm demands that you use your higher mind to steady yourself in the immediate aftermath of adversity. As such, it is perhaps the most personal phase in the nondirectional cycle of Leadership Resilience in Action. Despite its personal nature, your ability to stay calm is quite visible to those you lead, and it sets an emotional tone that empowers you and others. As with all the actions in the cycle, you will return to Stay Calm again and again as you respond to disruptive change.

FIRST DO NOTHING

Some people might think that "doing nothing" is inappropriately passive and, well, wimpy. This is because in order to assure our survival we are born with the powerful urge to vigilantly monitor and react to changes around us (Ariely, 2010). Therefore, when we do not react immediately to disruptive change, it makes us edgy: We think we are not doing our job. Worse, either real or imagined, we worry that doing nothing in place of reacting causes others to suspect we are not up to the demands of leadership.

Doing nothing is not taking the easy way out. According to behavioral economist Dan Ariely (2010), in fact, the automatic reactions and impulses we initially feel in the face of adversity (here I am referring to leadership challenges, not a crisis or emergency situation) could be exactly the wrong response. Ariely says when we find ourselves in a fix, we rifle our minds for "a precedent among past actions without regard to whether a decision was made in emotional or unemotional circumstances." This means that if we behaved a certain way in the past, as a victim of our own emotions, we are likely to behave that same way in the future even when our reaction and the current situation are mismatched. We are wired to react and act out habits and emotional patterns that may or may not be useful but that fit like a comfortable pair of shoes. Resisting the urge to react from the past is what makes doing nothing so challenging for most of us.

Doing nothing is emotionally and cognitively demanding and is a hallmark of leadership resilience. While less resilient leaders become frenetic or withdraw in the face of disruptive change, resilient leaders first allow themselves time to absorb the information. For example, Superintendent Dave Sholes told me about the time a bus driver let a distressed student out to use the restroom at a house along the route from school to home. Naturally, when the community learned of the unorthodox stop, it responded with vocal concern: Had the child been allowed to go into the home of a stranger? Sholes cautioned against a rush to judgment and encouraged people to wait for the results of the investigation. In the end, it became clear that the driver let the child off the bus to use the restroom at the home of a classmate whose parent supervised. The driver waited for the child who, much relieved, re-boarded the bus. Sholes said, "I'm not saying it was right for the driver to stop, but leaders who react to everything miss the opportunity to let new information emerge. Unless we're talking about a crisis, I wait and watch and listen. Sometimes what seemed to be a problem really isn't at all—or if there is a problem the new information helps me make a better decision."

Regulate Your Emotions to Serve Others

Neurologically, during this pause, resilient leaders reroute their emotional responses back to the thinking part of the brain where a dose of rationality is injected into the mix. This neural pause empowers leaders to actively resist the automatic reactions that arise in their agitated minds.

After a round of budget-trimming initiatives, Principal Riley had to break some tough news to his faculty: Half of the instructional coaching team would be reassigned to classroom teaching positions, replacing a number of teachers who were retiring from the district. Although Riley knew all along that instructional coaching could end up on the chopping block, he truly believed its positive track record of improving teaching through job-embedded professional development would preserve funding. While sitting in his office absorbing the news, Riley was gripped by a series of emotional reactions. From despair over the loss of support to key teachers who were just beginning to respond to coaching, to trepidation over having to mollify the teacher's union, to anxiety about having to break the news to the instructional coaches themselves and help them transform their roles and their perspectives, Riley knew the aftermath of this change would be difficult for many to accept. He lamented, how do we move forward when circumstances outside our control continually set us back?

Riley began to strategize how to present the news first to his administrative team and instructional coaches, and then to the rest of the faculty. Knowing that people follow his emotional lead, Riley thought about how he could simultaneously acknowledge the loss while projecting an appropriate amount of what he calls "can-doism." "After all," Riley explains, "how can I call myself a leader if I'm not helping people see how they can move forward?"

Regulating one's emotions is not the same thing as being morosely stoic, eerily calm, void of feeling, or sentimentally flat. To do so would devalue the real emotions people feel in the face of disruptive change and would undermine relationships and action in the new reality. (Think of how upset people were with Queen Elizabeth when she did not immediately express sadness when Princess Diana died in 1997. Conversely, think of how people—no matter what their political affiliation—appreciated President Obama's and New Jersey Governor Christie's united compassion for communities hit by Hurricane Sandy in 2012, ultimately motivating them toward hope and positive action.) Michigan superintendent Mark Bielang agrees. He says, "Everyone looks to leadership to see what your reactions are and then they act accordingly." When one of the district school buses was in an accident, for example, Bielang recognized that he had to "show up and stay calm when others were not." Compare this response to a different occasion when he had to deliver the eulogy at a faculty member's memorial service. Bielang said, "There are other times when you have to show a different emotion when the context and environment is appropriate to show sadness, for example, that gives permission for others to show sadness too. This puts healing in motion."

The Latin root of the word emotion is *emovere*—something that sets the mind in motion. Leaders who are weak in regulating their emotions are often seized by feelings that overpower them and catalyze a limited range of response. As we know from experts in neurology and psychology, emotions are contagious. In groups, the person displaying the strongest emotions sets the tone for others, but on teams and in organizations, the most powerful person in the group such as the designated leader sets the emotional tone (Goleman, 2011). Leaders who are overcome by emotions such as fear, anger, impatience, and pride, for example, experience a diminished or skewed sense of empowerment and efficacy, which they transmit to others (Caruso & Salovey, 2004).

Leaders carry a great responsibility: Not only do they set the emotional tone for the organization in times of turbulence, but they must discern and show the *appropriate* emotion—the one that helps people move forward, that helps them heal, that allows them to embrace the reality of the situation, that draws them into new realities. For example, in the aftermath of the tragic shootings at Sandy Hook Elementary School in 2012, Connecticut superintendent Pam Auburn, said, "For the parents and grandparents just struggling to drop their students off at school, I hold back my tears. When they see that the leaders are calm, they know they can depend on you no matter what happens." Robert Dubick, a New York superintendent, agrees that leaders need to monitor their emotions in order to positively affect others. He says, "You have to first acknowledge the situation. Then you have to ask yourself if what you're going to say will bring you closer to people or increase the distance between you and them. You have to ask, 'what do I want to have happen, what is it that others need from me at this particular time?'"

Consider the statements below that present emotions demonstrated by the leader and the possible positive responses they could catalyze in others:

- Leaders who show a sense of *humor* when recognizing or acknowledging a mistake catalyze *creativity* instead of fear in others.
- Leaders who express *sadness* activate *healing* for others.
- Leaders who display *enthusiasm* mobilize a sense of *possibility* in others.
- Leaders who show *gratitude* catalyze *efficacy* in others.
- Leaders who express *hope* increase *motivation* in others.
- Leaders who *resist nostalgia* help people express *new visions*.
- Leaders who express *confidence* invite others to *learn*.
- Leaders who authentically *comfort* others help them to *listen to and absorb information*.
- Leaders who are *compassionate* help *reduce isolation* for others.

The ability to stay calm first requires heightened awareness of one's own urge to react with familiar emotional responses that may not, in fact, initiate the most helpful set of actions for bouncing forward. Leaders who stay calm mindfully regulate their emotions in order to produce helpful emotions and actions in others. Resilient leaders tend to look at each fresh crisis with interest as opposed to judgment. They are less likely to see trouble as catastrophes and are more likely to say things like, *well isn't this interesting?* Perhaps they would even go so far as to allow they are in a "fine kettle of fish." But they often do nothing, at least for a little while. When they do take action, it usually results in a good outcome with concern for others as well as for themselves.

SUMMARY

When resilient leaders begin the cycle of Leadership Resilience in Action, they remain calm and alert, which sets an empowering emotional tone for others to follow.

ACTIVITIES AND QUESTIONS FOR STUDY GROUPS AND TEAMS

1. With a particular challenge from your leadership work in mind, and as you reflect on the content in this chapter, what will you draw from the leadership resilience-enabling capacities of Relationships, Resonance, and Renewal, and how do you need to bolster them?

   The leadership challenge I'm thinking of is:

   In order to help myself and others stay calm I need to draw on these ideas from the three leadership resilience enablers:

   • Relationships:

   • Resonance:

   • Renewal:

2. What would it feel like for you to actually have the strength to do nothing when what you really want to do is react?

3. Make a list of all the emotions you can think of, both helpful and destructive. Then, thinking of a specific leadership challenge either from the past or present, write down the impact of that emotion, if you were to exhibit it, on the people you lead.

4. Practice resilience on the small losses you face every day in your personal and work life. You know what I mean: when you miss a green light, lose your cell phone, lock yourself out of the house, or get a flat tire on your bike in the middle of long ride. When you miss an important call, when others are late for a meeting you planned, when a deadline is moved up in your calendar, when an additional piece of information is requested at the last minute. These frequent and annoying events, which are part and parcel to the daily churn of life, provide plenty of low-stakes opportunities to practice and strengthen the cycle of resilience in action. Every time you

respond resiliently, beginning with Stay Calm to these low-level disruptions, you retrain your brain for more resilience when the big disruptions occur.

5. For one week, make a note in your calendar, plan book, or journal whenever you feel upset or catch yourself saying something you later regret. Importantly, the faster you recover from a state of feeling hijacked by your emotions, the more resilient you are (Davidson et al., 2003; Goleman, 2011). With a friend, partner, or leadership coach, reflect on the event:

- What were the triggers?
- How long did it take you to recover?
- Did you do anything specific to recover?
- What were you aware of as it was happening?
- How did it affect the next thing you had to do that day?

6. Ask yourself if your typical reaction or the way you feel like responding will move you closer to people and toward the vision of the organization, or further away. If it does not, count to 10 and then think of another option.

7. Take a couple of breaths. Look at the bigger picture in addition to the scene right in front of you. Instead of responding negatively, actually say out loud: "Well, isn't that interesting."

8. Consider what would be the exact opposite of your usual reaction and try that first. See what happens.

9. Choose to be a leader. In other words, step up and resonate a demeanor that draws out the best in others.

10. Learn "mindfulness," a technique you practice much like meditation, to train the brain to register and fully focus on events in the present moment, without reacting (Goleman, 2011). Mindfulness practice consists of sitting quietly for a period of time while focusing on your breath. When thoughts come to you, go ahead and notice them but then return your focus to your breath. Over time, the ability to resist impulsive reactions transfers to the workplace. You'll know you are getting good at this when you feel a reduction in your overall level of stress.

7 Carry On

St. Francis of Assisi was once asked what he would do if he knew he had only one more day to live. He said, "I would continue to hoe my garden."

Reminder: As you read this chapter, note where the ideas and strategies presented draw on the leadership resilience-enabling capacities of Relationships, Resonance, and Renewal. Then, at the end of the chapter, write down what you want to learn about or experience in order to bolster the capacities so that you are better able to respond in the aftermath of adversity and disruptive change.

hile writing this book, two significant events took place in my life, one at a national level and one within my own family. The first one, the December 14, 2012, murders at Sandy Hook Elementary School in Connecticut, unfolded in horrifying detail across the television and Internet. The second event, on January 7, 2013, was the quiet passing of my father-in-law, a brilliant, kind, and humorous man who served as dean of the medical school at the University of New Mexico from 1972 to 1994. For me, both events created a poignant backdrop for conversations about resilience, and both events underscore some of the finer points of leadership resiliency in action.

CARRY ON

This chapter illuminates what resilient leaders do to carry on in the face of adversity, challenge, loss, and disruptive change. Yet, how, as in the case of Sandy Hook, does a person—not to mention a whole community—continue to function when children and faculty are unthinkably killed within their schools and classrooms? The answer, of course, is not easy. But we can look to the magical qualities of ordinary resilience, which helps us to suss out the exacting requirements of leadership resilience.

Maintain Momentum

Perhaps the only thing more unsettling than disruptive change is realizing that while your attention and energy was diverted, the rest of the organization fell apart. For example, when my father-in-law passed away, and as our family navigated the rough terrain of grief, we instinctively carried out common yet important routines. One of my sisters-in-law took over dishwasher loading while the other coordinated our meals. My husband and I hauled trash, and we all took turns with the washer and dryer. Neighbors and friends brought us food so we would remember to eat, and they sat with us and shared memories and stories that made us smile and laugh. These simple and ordinary tasks sustained our momentum. They facilitated our personal resilience by keeping us moving forward into the next day, and the next day, and the next day, and they reminded us that life is both beautifully humble and profound.

In the aftermath of adversity, leaders cannot afford to allow routines to stall, as this only compounds disruption and makes stepping forward into the new reality that much more difficult. While in the raw stage of change and loss, the routines that maintain organizational operations also sustain momentum for the organization. In the context of Leadership Resilience in Action, to Carry On means that leaders must see to the operations of the organization, to keep things running where they can and where they must. No matter what else has happened, buses still need to operate, cafeteria food still needs to be served, and students still need to learn.

For example, Principal Riley was in the middle of conducting informal observations and feedback sessions with the instructional coaches when he learned that half of them would be reassigned. For a split second he thought of abandoning the effortful and time-consuming process. But because he was building a culture that valued learning from change, he realized that dropping his commitment to this aspect of supervision would send the wrong message to the coaches and to the rest of the faculty. Instead of getting off track, Riley saw the observation and feedback process as an opportunity to learn even more about what it means to be a great instructional coach. Knowledge about what works in a reduced budget, Riley explained to his coaching team, would likely inspire novel approaches for supporting teachers that would serve them well when the budget was restored and they could put coaching back on the table.

Ask for Help

Resilient leaders have cultivated a robust network of diverse relationships, poised to help them when needed. When it comes to sustaining the momentum of the organization, asking for their help is a wise move. After the school shooting in Newtown, Connecticut, for example, Superintendent Janet Robinson asked the state department to send her a retired superintendent who would be willing and able to run previously scheduled meetings for district committees so that she could focus entirely on leading in the aftermath of this tragedy.

But asking for help should not be limited to times of crisis and tragedy. Like most school districts across the country, the Storey County School District in Idaho, led by 2013 Utah Superintendent of the Year, Dr. Robert Slaby, faced steep budget cuts. Determined to trim the budget without compromising student learning, Slaby scrutinized the district's operational processes and sought innovative solutions to contain costs. Among the many strategies the district put in place included the donation of a solar array to one of the elementary schools from business partner Black Rock Solar. Slaby understands, however, that relationships that benefit the district must also be reciprocal. With the solar array project, for example, not only will the elementary school save energy costs, but Black Rock Solar gets to provide an alternative power source to the community and green jobs to local workers. The beauty of asking for help is that when it is given and received, important relationships become stronger and resilience increases.

Giving and Gratitude

Asking for help is a reciprocal proposition with benefits to the giver and receiver alike. When you ask for what you need, you get better at asking for what you need—something many leaders are not good at doing. In addition, you experience the emotion of gratitude, which is a source of renewal and energy. Simultaneously, the other parties gain the experience of *giving*.

Here is an example: Reflecting on his wise decision to hire Jody Leinenwever to take over as assistant superintendent of human resources, for example, Ron Richards told me, "I was the business manager before I was superintendent, so I was not expert in personnel matters. So I brought Jody in—I wanted her to teach me everything she knew about HR, and in spite of the fact that she told me this was a temporary position for her, my request invigorated her—and she stayed and together we went on to do great things."

Mitigate Suffering for Others

In order to carry on in the aftermath of adversity, leaders sometimes have to take steps to release people from what they believe is holding them back. Most people are stronger than they believe they are, but some situations or a compounded number of disruptive events can push people to the edges of their resilience. In the midst of disruptive change, you can make it easier for people to eventually bounce forward by taking steps to mitigate the pain of change.

To illustrate this point, I find it helpful to understand an engineering term known as the modulus of resilience. The modulus of resilience describes the extent to which solid structures, such as steel beams, can bend without becoming permanently deformed. Although steel beams that shore up skyscrapers are very strong, they also flex a little within an acceptable range, without becoming damaged. When the range is exceeded, however, even steel will snap.

In organizations, people usually display the limits of their resilience by resisting change. Sadly, their resistance holds them back from participating in emerging opportunities and limits their professional and personal experiences—the very conditions that make work and life interesting and enriching. Resilient leaders care about these colleagues, and they look for ways to mitigate their discomfort without compromising the forward motion of the organization. Mark Bielang describes it this way: "We acknowledge people's fears but we stick with what we know is the right thing to do. We label the fears and then find ways to make it better. We continue on by giving people the support they need."

The *symptoms* of resistance are usually visible: people complain, disengage, miss meetings, withhold requested information, or they simply ignore responsibilities. In times of disruptive change, symptoms of resistance signal that resilience for individuals and the organization is in jeopardy. Rather than focus on the symptoms, however, leaders need to understand that mitigation has much to do with responding swiftly and appropriately to the emotional needs of the people involved (Tedlow, 2010). In complex organizations, for example, emotional needs include fears of incompetency in the unknown future state, stress over misinformation or loss of favored resources, sadness about losing key relationships, and anxiety over misinformation or incomplete information.

At the root of these emotions is loss of attachment: the state of emotional distress experienced by people when the structures or people or cultures they have come to lean on for support disappear (Grady & Grady, 2012). Writing about organizational change in general, Grady and Grady suggest that substitutions for what was lost help people regain a sense of stability as they ease into change. They write, "those replacements could be a leader, a favored object, a method of communication, a continuing education series, a technology, a colleague, a culture, or any combination of these items" (p. 86).

Mitigation is also about rolling up your leadership sleeves and learning in the new reality alongside others. Bielang gives the example of the flurry of new teacher evaluation development going on across the country. He said, "Yes, the new state teacher evaluation system is a change and it will take more of our time, but I'm right there, learning with everyone else. We are in this together."

WAYS RESILIENT LEADERS MITIGATE THE LOSSES THAT DISRUPTIVE CHANGE BRINGS

Leaders that take action to lessen the harshness and intensity of pain that accompanies disruptive change reveal an important sensitivity to the modulus of resilience. Here are some ideas:

- Be active and visible in your leadership.
- Provide focused professional development so people can develop needed new skills.
- Provide timely, accurate, and frequent information, even if it is only to say that new information is unavailable.
- Assure that front-line leaders advocate for forward motion.
- Give solace and comfort. Just listen.
- Use humor respectfully. One principal put a big jar of coins in the faculty lounge that said, "Afraid of change? Leave yours here!"
- Involve people in designing the new pathways forward.
- Sit and listen to people who are most impacted or most invested in what was lost.
- Help people see their role in the new reality and support them in connecting their new roles with their passions.
- Reduce low-priority demands—take things off their plate where you can.
- Spontaneously jump in and work alongside people.
- Connect people with each other for mentoring, coaching, and friendships.

SUMMARY

In the immediate aftermath of disruptive change, resilient leaders make sure that the organization continues to function. Doing so sustains momentum and makes it easier for people to bounce forward. In order to Carry On, leaders call on their network of relationships for support, and they take steps to mitigate the pain of change for others.

ACTIVITIES AND QUESTIONS FOR STUDY GROUPS AND TEAMS

1. With a particular challenge from your leadership work in mind, and as you reflect on the content in this chapter, what will you draw from the leadership resilience-enabling capacities of Relationships, Resonance, and Renewal, and how do you need to bolster them?

   The leadership challenge I'm thinking of is:

   In order to help myself and others Carry On, I need to draw on these ideas from the three leadership resilience-enabling capabilities:

   • Relationships:

   • Resonance:

   • Renewal:

2. With one or more specific challenges in mind, who do you want to ask for help? How can you reciprocate?

3. What functions within the organization (your classroom, your school, district, community) run smoothly? Which ones do not function well unless they have a lot of guidance and oversight? Build in redundancies now to keep the more "needy" functions operating smoothly in the event of disruptive change.

4. Who has the skills needed to jump in and cover for other colleagues as needed? Where do you have helpful redundancies in skills, people, and resources?

5. Thinking of the people you work with, what do they value in times of change? Go back and read the section in this chapter titled "Ways Resilient Leaders Mitigate the Losses That Disruptive Change Brings" and identify several strategies that fit your culture.

8 Accept the New Reality

Reminder: As you read this chapter, note where the ideas and strategies presented draw on the leadership resilience-enabling capacities of Relationships, Resonance, and Renewal. Then, at the end of the chapter, write down what you want to learn about or experience in order to bolster the capacities so that you are better able to respond in the aftermath of adversity and disruptive change.

At some point, in response to disruptive change, resilient leaders take the first visible steps toward the new reality and they beckon others to come along. The new reality includes the social, emotional, political, cultural, professional, and personal facets and forces, both negative and positive, that come into view when the smoke begins to clear. Many people find the prospect of stepping into the unknown territory of new realities terribly frightening; leaders are not exempt from feelings of fear and anxiety. But resilient leaders understand that debilitating emotions and perceptions prevent them from meeting the demands of leadership.

ADJUST YOUR PERSPECTIVE

New realities require leaders to think accurately about the implications of adversity—about what will happen from this point forward into the foreseeable future (Reivich & Shatté, 2002). The ability to de-escalate adversities by adjusting and revising your perspective in order to think accurately is a sure sign of resilience. While reframing one's perspective promotes individual resiliency, leaders have the extra requirement of helping others see clearly yet optimistically toward a future they will need to create.

Consider the story of Lee (not his real name), a novice principal who is low in leadership resilience. Lee tends to perceive disruptive change as personal assaults against his leadership style and ability. He takes everything personally and blows up easily. His staff whispers among themselves that he has a short fuse. Lee's underlying assumption is that disruptions, setbacks, and losses reflect his inability to lead. Moreover, he projects this assumption onto others, believing that they also attribute disruptive changes in the environment to his wanting leadership skills. As a result, Lee comes off as defensive and he misses many opportunities to transform adversity into growth.

For example, when the climate survey was returned from the school community with relatively low marks in the domain of "communication," Lee decided it meant that people did not appreciate the good news he always shared about student progress in his newsletters and presentations. Laboring under a skewed perspective, Lee angrily told his supervisor, "If parents want me to communicate more, by golly, I'll make sure they know they are not pulling their weight in this school."

Lee's response is decidedly uncharacteristic of leadership resilience. If he were able to reframe his perspective, Lee would see that most of the information that disrupts his equilibrium and causes him to react defensively is not about him personally at all, but is helpful feedback signaling opportunity. Ironically, Lee creates most of the mischief and angst he later feels he has to defend himself against. Let's take a look at some of the many ways Lee could more positively reframe his perspective about the climate survey:

1. We are fortunate our parents responded to the climate survey. This means they value communication between school and home.

2. Two-way communication is an important variable for student success. I'm eager to learn new ways to accomplish this.

3. Our parents value communication with us, and they want more of it in order to be of support to their students.

4. We conduct community surveys in order to improve our practices. We value and respect all responses and can learn from each and every responder.

Equipped with any one of the reframed perspectives above, Lee would have a variety of leadership responses at his disposal that elude him under his original paradigm. Instead of responding with disrespect and disdain (not qualities of leadership), Lee would extend gratitude, seek innovative ideas, set an example for the rest of the faculty, and make changes that could have a profound effect on student achievement in addition to school and community relationships.

When it comes to accepting the new reality and setting the stage for positive action to follow, leaders who reframe unhelpful and maladaptive perspectives change the trajectory of events to follow. As Seligman (1991) puts it, "Our thoughts are not merely reactions to events; they change what ensues" (p. 7). Understanding that our thoughts and reactions create the future could make some leaders hesitant in making decisions. But Superintendent Bettye Ray reminds us, "Yes, we have to grapple with decisions we make, but when they are guided by a healthy perspective we must move on."

Contrast Lee's story with that of Robert Haley, a superintendent in Northern California, who quite literally stepped into a new reality when during a recent school year the new high school principal he hired the summer before abruptly left the district under a cloud of controversy. Feeling an acute sense of accountability, Haley assumed the principal's duties in addition to his. Haley told me, "The reality is, I hired someone who was not up to the job. It doesn't matter that everyone, including me, originally believed he was up to the job; in the end he was not, and I am accountable." Haley did not spend a lot of time in nostalgia or denial. Nor did he describe feeling victimized. Instead he added an assistant principal to assist him and began the work of stabilizing the learning environment. Haley is realistic: He knows he cannot serve both roles well forever, and he also knows he needs to take time to renew. But until Haley hires a new principal, his proactive perspective signals resilience and engenders confidence throughout the school community.

Sue Page and Maggie Cuellar, who are both area superintendents in Alief, Texas, support and supervise the principals in their district. They have seen a lot of school leaders over the years and have made some keen observations about how leaders overcome negative and unhelpful perspectives. They suggest that fear of rejection is at the root of what on the surface looks like defiance, negativity, passivity, laziness, aggressiveness, rashness, or what have you. Doreen Corrente, executive director of the Rhode Island Center for School Leadership, also names fear as an undermining force—especially in districts where the union and the administration seem to work at cross-purposes. Corrente says feeling fear is as true for teacher leaders who have watched others endure ostracism or criticism (or both) for trying something new, as it is for administrators. "I knew teacher leaders who did not want to be acknowledged or receive kudos because they did not want to stand out. Sadly, this sort of climate discourages many people from stepping into leadership roles they would be great for; they see the difficulties and they decide it is better to not rock the boat."

For Page and Cuellar, understanding that fear debilitates resilient leadership means that part of their job is to help leaders cultivate trust—trust in themselves and in others—and to learn how to build trust with their faculties and staffs. Corrente adds that a true cultural shift from fear to trust will not happen unless the central administration is also committed to the process. Corrente says, "If it doesn't happen at the top, then it is easy to see school-level leaders focus only on doing their own thing."

In their article "Mindfulness, Hope and Compassion: A Leader's Road Map to Renewal" (2006), McKee, Johnston, and Massimilian say that trust emerges when leaders are mindful enough to ask themselves questions about their behavior that put them in touch with the "subtle messages" of the people they lead—questions such as "Am I acting in concert with my values? Am I the leader I aspire to be? How am I doing managing the stress of my current situation? How are my key people feeling these days" (p. 3). Ultimately, as Page, Cuellar, and Corrente have observed, trust diminishes fear, which in turn reduces the stress that make leaders negative, dissonant, and withdrawn.

RESIST NOSTALGIA

Disruptive change is not only unexpected, but more importantly, it is *change*—and as everyone knows, even planned change can be troublesome. Change thrusts people into transition—that disorienting space between the known and unknown (Bridges, 1980) where the old rules, assumptions, and algorithms for "how we do things around here" no longer apply. This is a shaky time for people, and nostalgia for what was lost will tug mightily at their hearts. Less resilient leaders rail against change. Oddly enough, they do so even when what they had before the change *also* caused them dismay. "After all," says retired superintendent John Aycock, "Resilience is nothing if it is not about hope, about looking forward. And what is leadership if it is not about moving forward?" Leaders who glamorize the past or denigrate the potential of the new reality hold their colleagues and the organization back. Nostalgia has the power to negate resilience.

Leaders taking others into a new future cannot indulge in debilitating longing for the past. In fact, they must actively challenge organizational structures that work to preserve the past and therefore work against acceptance of the new reality. Not to do so sustains cultures that are toxic to new realities. Consider, for example, the glaring mismatch between vision and culture in districts that say they want to close achievement gaps for economically disadvantaged students but then continue to place these students in classes with the most inexperienced teachers.

As Peter Drucker is known to have said, "culture eats strategy for breakfast." This means that even as leaders seek pathways forward into new realities, they must simultaneously help the culture evolve. What a tall order! Resilient leaders can begin this challenging work by engaging others in the review of existing policies and past decisions, and begin to reshape or excise those that no longer apply (Hamel, 2009).

Resilient leaders also resist nostalgia by describing the new reality in present tense and vivid detail, taking care to identify what still exists from the past and what is new and good. These details are new bearings; they help people find their way, and they give them stability and courage to respond. At no time is accepting new realities more important than when disruptive events make their way into the newspapers, on television, and on the Internet. Many times, what the media considers newsworthy are comments the leader has no control over, such as those made by board members, parents, and students. Superintendent Randy Poe says, "Under these circumstances do not deviate from the mission." Superintendent Daniel Boyd adds, "When you are clear on the details, it is important to be honest about whatever happened and then pull people together and let the mission guide you toward the best response."

SUMMARY

Resilient leaders step confidently in the new realities that emerge in the aftermath of disruptive change. These leaders are adept at adjusting their perspective in order to see the opportunities in adversity and in resisting the powerful force of nostalgia. They are especially vigilant about resisting the temptation to let nostalgia for the past creep into their conversations with others. Instead, they bring their absorbed insights from the past forward, and they immerse themselves in apprehending new realities through fresh eyes.

ACTIVITIES AND QUESTIONS FOR
STUDY GROUPS AND TEAMS

1. With a particular challenge from your leadership work in mind, and as you reflect on the content in this chapter, what will you draw from the leadership resilience-enabling capacities of Relationships, Resonance, and Renewal, and how do you need to bolster them?

   The leadership challenge I'm thinking of is:

   In order to help myself and others Accept the New Reality, I need to draw on these ideas from the three leadership resilience-enabling capacities:

   • Relationships:

   • Resonance:

   • Renewal:

2. What do you say to yourself and what do you hear others say that signify a nostalgic view of the past?

3. What has been "the good" that has come to you from the last "new reality" you stepped into?

4. Who or what would give you courage in new realities?

9

Want
Something More

Reminder: As you read this chapter, note where the ideas and strategies presented draw on the leadership resilience-enabling capacities of Relationships, Resonance, and Renewal. Then, at the end of the chapter, write down what you want to learn about or experience in order to bolster the capacities so that you are better able to respond in the aftermath of adversity and disruptive change.

As people begin to accept new realities, they enter an intriguing phase of creating a future that leverages the opportunities—the silver linings of disruptive change. I'll give you a personal example: While I was working on another writing project, my computer crashed and my files were unrecoverable. To add insult to injury, I had not set up my backup drive properly (the dog had not heard such language before, nor has he since). As a researcher, writer, and small-business owner, this means I lost an enormous amount of intellectual property. More than a year's worth of writing and work disappeared into thin air. There was nothing left for me to do but recreate the book that was due in four weeks, and begin to develop from scratch everything I needed to do my research and work. At first losing my files felt like a horrible, horrible tragedy. But as I started to strategize my recovery, I had this incredible insight: Even though I had evolved as a researcher, writer, businessperson, and leader, for the sake of efficiency, I relied on old tools, forms, processes, and policies that did not reflect my growth. In other words, for the sake of efficiency, I was settling for mediocrity. Until the "tragedy" of my computer crash, I might not have taken time to update and transform the way I do my work.

WANT SOMETHING MORE

The losses that make resilience possible also provide the necessary "breakdowns" that press leaders to imagine new potentials within themselves and the system. In organizations, resilient leaders have a knack for helping people emerge from difficulties yearning for something more. This phase in the Leadership Resilience in Action cycle is Want Something More. Leaders enact this phase by asking questions and listening, and by keeping the vision of the organization front and center.

Ask Thought Leadership Questions

In the context of leadership resilience, wanting something more requires people to move toward new realities that challenge the previous status quo. This is the time in the change process when people recognize they have a voice in creating the new or polished organizational vision and the pathways forward. At this point, resilient leaders ask powerful questions that get people talking about the possibilities they see in the aftermath of disruptive change.

"Thought leadership questions" (Allison et al., 2012) is a term I coined in my book *Renewal Coaching Fieldbook: How Effective Leaders Sustain Meaningful Change.* In the *Renewal Coaching Fieldbook* I write that thought leadership questions "elevate discussions between people in the organization away from habitual ways of thinking that lead to cliché ideas that rarely provide inspirational thought and toward those 'aha!' lightbulb moments that quicken innovation" (p. 18). In the aftermath of disruptive change, resilient leaders get together with people and ask questions that invite them to have a say in designing the future. Questions that either impose or remove limitations, called "constraining questions" (Dyer, Gregersen, & Christensen, 2011), provide you with a specific tool for encouraging people to imagine possibilities and take them beyond their fears.

Constraining Questions

Constraining questions are "what if" questions that either impose or eliminate constraints as a way to catalyze innovation. To *impose* constraints, for example, ask questions like this: "If state testing did not exist, what else would we do to know if all students were learning?" Or, "What if funding for technology ended? How would we assure that all students had a handheld smart device?" Or, "How might we get senior citizens and people without children to visit and volunteer in our schools?" Questions that *eliminate* constraints sound like this: "If we did not have common standards, what would you want students to learn?" Or, "What if every student was required to attend a post-secondary learning option? How would it change our course offerings?" Or, "What if we were comfortable with students using smartphones in class? What would be different about how we teach?" Or, "What if everyone believed that all students can learn no matter what their ethnicity or socioeconomic status?"

Constraining questions have the unique ability to cast the mind toward exploration as opposed to limitations and, similar to brainstorming, they have a way of surfacing surprising ideas. When you ask constraining questions to encourage people in the organization to share their thoughts, feelings, and ideas with you after disruptive change, you invite them to have a voice in honing the revised vision. Naturally, after you ask a question, you must fall to silence so people can respond. When you *really* listen, not only will you learn what stakeholders think is now possible in the organization, but as they hear themselves speak, your stakeholders will learn about themselves. As they hear the ideas they come up with in response to the constraining questions you ask, they may be surprised to discover just how resilient and creative they are.

Listen. Just Listen

In the aftermath of adversity, the altered landscape of the organization often requires new decisions. Sometimes policies and procedures need to be revised. Other times resources need to be moved around and cultural practices about how people interact with each other need to change. In order to make new decisions, leaders certainly expose themselves to large quantities of data, evidence, and information, which they use well in the decision-making process. But resilient leaders go a step further: They listen to the stories people want to tell them about what they personally need in order to bounce forward. Stories go above and beyond hard facts and reveal the heart as well as the mind. Story collections illuminate the field surrounding decisions, making clear the best course of action (Allison et al., 2012). The listening required to attend to these stories is based in discipline and compassion (Nichols, 1995).

Kim Klein, who is a leader in nonprofit work here in the Bay Area where I live, sees listening as being key to achieving buy-in. In the *Renewal Coaching Fieldbook,* I wrote that Kim told me, "People don't form opinions if no one asks them what they think and then listen to them. People have to hear their own voice and then see if they like themselves—if what they hear themselves say out loud really is what they feel" (p. 171).

Teacher leader Jonathan Sperling, of North High School in Torrance, California, discovered the power of listening firsthand when he realized that a growing group of students were becoming less and less invested in their own education. The moment that galvanized Sperling to action came when he saw a group of students high-fiving each other for receiving failing grades. When he asked the students to explain this celebration of failure, they told him they felt that the adults seemed not to really care whether or not they succeeded, so why should they?

Out of this crisis, Sperling and his colleagues worked with students, asking them, "What would it look like if everyone in our school cared?" Sperling and his colleagues wanted the students to be the architects of the schoolwide program that eventually came to be called "I Care." When they asked students to write their ideas down, they received pages and pages of their thoughts. But Sperling also had a large group of students who asked if they could talk about it. They told Sperling, "We have ideas now! Can we talk with you about it now?" Sperling told me that the most powerful ideas came when students talked with each other while he just listened. "The students revealed they wanted to recognize each other in ways different from race. This was exciting to me. I had no idea they were thinking this way" (Allison et al., 2012, p. 172).

An Underrated Leadership Skill

Listening is an underrated leadership skill; everyone thinks they are experts at listening, so they do not prioritize learning how to listen *well.* What prevents leaders from listening? Some leaders believe that unless they are dispensing wisdom, advice, and opinions, they are not doing their job. Other leaders fear wrong-headed ideas will prevail unless their voices dominate conversations. These leaders are well meaning—they use their words to demonstrate leadership, and certainly, when it comes to leading words matter. Powerful words that inspire others, however, arise out of listening longer and deeper than what is usual and even comfortable.

In the aftermath of disruptive change, listening is a critical tool that resilient leaders use to help people hear themselves think out loud about what they want in the new reality. Superintendent Randy Poe says it best: "When you listen, you show that you are willing to put yourself out there and that you are listening because you want to take action that people have had a hand in guiding. This means that even if they don't agree with you 100%, they know you listened to their input and it helps them manage the turbulence they feel as you move forward." Listening in the aftermath of adversity signals a prelude to action. It begins to make clear the way forward.

Purpose and Vision

Shared visions draw people into the future and establish high levels of commitment. They are a powerful source of inspiration and hope. Especially during times of disruptive change, however, new decisions are called for— many of which affect the tactics and strategies in play to achieve the vision. And some adversities reach beyond the strategy level to alter the current organizational vision itself.

Although they are relatively stable, organizational visions *do* change, often due to the disruption created when we learn a better way of accomplishing our goals. Think if you can, for example, back to the days when teachers and administrators were unaware of the power of collaboration and teaming. In those days, working under the assumption that teaching was an act carried out in isolation, most education visions did not include vivid descriptions about learning organizations and professional learning communities. Now, hardly a school vision exists that doesn't reference collaboration in some way.

Organizational visions also change when disruption discredits the assumptions they relied on. Consider, for example, the powerful effect of United States Public Law 94-142 back in the 1970s, which rightfully required schools to revise their vision to include a free and appropriate education for students with special learning needs and then deliver strategies to make it happen. Pervasive innovations in the world around us also alter visions. New technologies, for example, make it possible for learners of all ages to learn anytime and anywhere outside of the four walls of the school building.

In the long run, of course, organizations that embrace changes to the vision are more sustainable than those that do not. Evolving visions keep organizations in touch with the changing needs of stakeholders and make them relevant. But in the short run, disruptions to strategies and organizational vision unmoor stakeholders. This is a particularly vulnerable time for leaders, says Sue Page, an area superintendent in Texas. Page says, "When new information suggests our vision needs 're-vision' or when the vision doesn't come about through the methods I expected it to, I have to ask myself, 'how open am I here?' You have to stay open and you have to release."

Resilient school leaders must become adept, therefore, at articulating the evolution of the organizational vision and the interplay between evolving visions and strategies. Whether it strikes at the heart of the organization's vision or not, disruptive change requires leaders and others to open themselves to new possibilities. This is what keeps the vision renewed and relevant, and it is what ultimately sustains the organization.

SUMMARY

In the aftermath of adversity or disruptive change, resilient leaders lead others to Want Something More. They elicit this response through asking thought leadership questions, listening, and keeping the purpose and evolving vision of the organization front and center.

ACTIVITIES AND QUESTIONS FOR
STUDY GROUPS AND TEAMS

1. With a particular challenge from your leadership work in mind, and as you reflect on the content in this chapter, what will you draw from the leadership resilience-enabling capacities of Relationships, Resonance, and Renewal, and how do you need to bolster them?

   The leadership challenge I'm thinking of is:

   In order to help myself and others Want Something More, I need to draw on these ideas from the three leadership resilience enablers:

   • Relationships:

   • Resonance:

   • Renewal:

2. Thinking of a particular challenge, adversity, or disruptive change currently facing you, write as many constraining thought leadership questions as you can about it. Once you produce your list of questions, make another list of the stakeholders to pose them to. Try a few out and see what happens. Reflect on the process and the outcome with a colleague, your coach, or your leadership team.

3. How does the specific challenge or adversity you are thinking of operate on the current vision or the strategies toward the vision? Are they in alignment with the current vision? Where do the current challenges call assumptions into question? Meet with a thought partner who will listen as you flesh this out.

4. What are all the positive possibilities in the new reality, as you see them?

5. How does the current vision in your organization usually evolve? Does it emerge out of crisis? Out of external demands such as rules and regulations? Out of opportunities that come along?

10 Instigate Adaptive Action

Action is the antidote to despair.

—Joan Baez

Reminder: As you read this chapter, note where the ideas and strategies presented draw on the leadership resilience-enabling capacities of Relationships, Resonance, and Renewal. Then, at the end of the chapter, write down what you want to learn about or experience in order to bolster the capacities so that you are better able to respond in the aftermath of adversity and disruptive change.

In the near aftermath of adversity, *action* is what makes leadership resilience so extraordinary. Action is bouncing forward. Different from the relative languorous run up to long-term strategic planning, disruptive change challenges leaders with a compressed amount of time to make a plan and take meaningful action. As such, resilient leaders have no other choice: If they want their organizations to bounce forward, they must take adaptive actions that produce valuable information about the best pathways forward.

INSTIGATE ADAPTIVE ACTION

Adaptive actions are not rash; they are coherent to the mission of the organization. But because they are born out of challenge and surprising change, they may be uncommon and are more likely to arise from your intuition and out of improvisation instead of a textbook. Their real value is that even when they create imperfect results or even go awry, adaptive action creates information that gets you closer to what *will* work. Simultaneously, adaptive action helps people find their feet within new realities and sometimes discover new passions within themselves.

Experiment

The authors of the book *The Innovator's DNA: Mastering the Five Skills of Disruptive Innovators* (Dyer, Gregersen, & Christensen, 2011) write about the lack of information available to leaders after disruptive change and when they are making decisions about how to respond. They write, "Often the only way to get the necessary data to move forward is to run the experiment" (Kindle Location 1883). These ideas are central to those of Donald Schön, the highly regarded expert in organizational learning who wrote about what it means to be a reflective practitioner. Describing the process of reflection in action, Schön writes in his seminal book, *The Reflective Practitioner: How Professionals Think in Action* (1983), "He carries out an experiment which serves to generate both a new understanding of the phenomenon and a change in the situation" (p. 68). Superintendent Rick Miller believes disruptive change stimulates innovation, and he is supportive of those who feel moved to design experiences that create insight. Miller told me, "I look for the passionate teacher who says, 'look I'd like to try this strategy or that approach here because I think it will make a difference.' If it goes well, this is the kind of teacher who can influence others and then we can bring the innovation to scale and help even more students."

Some leaders are paralyzed by the thought of taking action. What if they lead in the wrong direction? Ironically, in the absence of action and reflection on results, leaders have nothing to go on; they cannot correct a course they have not yet begun. Paralysis during defining moments signals nostalgia for a past reality that no longer exists. Therefore, when it comes to leading with resilience, pockets of spontaneous experimentation in the aftermath of loss makes a whole lot of sense.

Consider the story of Bernice, a principal who came up to me after a talk I gave on resilience in 2008. Bernice described losing the full-time resource teachers who met with students after their morning classes to reteach, reinforce, and review what they learned that day. The staff reduction was quite a blow not only to the morale of her faculty but also to the parents who were promised their students would receive extra support to help them catch up to their peers. Not wanting to let these students fall through the cracks, Bernice and her staff quickly patched together a schedule of support that had some students meeting with teachers during their free periods *before* students attended class. The faculty was naturally skeptical—wouldn't the delay between class time and review time simply be too long? But then something interesting happened. A few teachers decided to abandon the paradigm of review and reteach, and replace it with a paradigm of preview and pre-teach. In a matter of days, the students who attended the pre-teaching sessions started to do better and learn more in class. As time went on, these students also exhibited fewer behavior problems and said they liked school better. For Bernice's school, adaptive change opened the door to profound innovative change.

Inspired thought often arises, quite surprisingly, out of disruptive change and loss. In truth, leaders of complex systems never have as much control over how changes will affect the organization as they think they do. Resilient leaders understand that the only way to really know how the system will function after you modify it is to modify it. Then, observe what happens and use the resulting data to make mid-course corrections, decide what to remain committed to, and hone and refine the new approaches that emerge.

As we saw with Bernice's school, adaptive actions can be the start of something big—a new program, practice, or process. Other adaptive actions are subtle but produce important information that reveals the way forward. Here are a few examples of the types of adaptive action resilient leaders instigate not long after disruptive change. Notice that each of these examples naturally produce information that create understanding and could lead to excellent solutions—they each get the ball rolling:

- Examine and revise or remove unhelpful policies that prevent people from experimenting and taking risks.
- Make adaptations to the environment that create the *conditions* for success (physical space, time, people, tools).
- Tap different people and people in different fields for their ideas, resources, and talents.

- Remove rules and customs that prevent people from contributing.
- Introduce experiences that help people learn something difficult and crucial.
- Design a "work around" and show others how to use it.
- Fundamentally transform a belief or behavior in yourself.

Needless to say, courageous experimentation is daunting in organizations where the prevailing culture punishes "mistakes." Leaders who are serious about creating resilient organizations will make adaptive action a priority within the culture.

Stare Back at Fear

Arizona superintendent Ron Richards recalls the time he was caught off guard by a public vote in favor of consolidating the elementary and secondary school district in his area—districts that up until this point functioned completely independent of each other. Everyone was stunned by the vote, and everyone was afraid about how the reorganization would take place. Many wondered if they would still have jobs. Richards told me, "It was really hard to be positive, and it really took a toll on me. But because everyone was in turmoil, I knew I had to stand up and say 'everything will be fine.'"

Once Richards accepted the reality of the vote, he decided to take the lead. He established a committee comprised of all the other affected superintendents as well as others, and he agreed to head it up. Richards said, "This was one way I could reassure my stakeholders that I was involved and was proactive and could help us respond as things unfolded."

Astoundingly, four months in, irregularities in the election process came to light and the vote to consolidate districts was declared null and void. Everyone was relieved, of course, but Richards said the experience taught them not to take the community for granted or assume to know what they want. Richards said, "The result of what we learned is that although the elementary districts and the high school districts are separate, we needed to embrace a new business model; we needed to collaborate and communicate more about the needs of students, we needed to share resources, business processes, and data. We learned that what the community really wanted was greater efficiency and greater communication about their students."

Richards is adept at instigating adaptive action, which in this case led to tremendous opportunities within an entirely new paradigm. For many leaders, however, fear is a powerful emotion that interferes with their ability to think, make good decisions, and take adaptive action. Everyone feels fear, anger, jealousy, attachment, and other unhelpful emotions once in a while. But when these powerful emotions cause you to think small, become manipulative, and use others without giving back, they reduce the infinite possibilities of life and they rob you of resilience.

Daniel Goleman (2004) recounts a strategy for dealing with destructive emotions that Buddhist monk and author Matthieu Ricard calls "staring back." Ricard explains that when thoughts associated with fear and other destructive emotions begin, they usually spawn another thought and then another, until "our mental landscape becomes invaded by thoughts that solidify our anger or jealousy—and then it's too late. Just as when a spark of fire has set a whole forest on fire, we are in trouble" (p. 214). Leaders that learn to recognize resilience-inhibiting emotions and thoughts when they arise can also learn to interrupt their proliferation. Ricard says that staring back means that we first register the fact that we are in the grip of a powerful emotion, but we then stare it down with objectivity and reason.

You Have Skills

One of the easiest ways to get a grip on ourselves in the presence of fear is to remind ourselves that *we have skills*. If you haven't seen the movie *Napoleon Dynamite,* I recommend you do so this weekend for an excellent example of this resilience strategy in action. In the film (no spoiler alert here), you'll see the main character, Napoleon, and his buddy, Pedro—two awkward and alienated high schoolers—achieve unthinkable goals by reminding themselves they *have skills* and then using them in intrepid pursuit of their goals. They even lend their skills to each other and, in a line that delights my staff developer's heart, they cajole each other to "get some skills."

The point is that during times of unexpected change, even highly skilled, talented, and wise leaders can succumb to self-doubt. While knowing what you don't know is a strength, believing that you lack what you need to rise to the challenges before you is not. Resilient leaders remember they did not get this far in their career without learning a thing or two about how the world works, and even though the new situation is different they will not be bullied by fear of the unknown.

DEFINING MOMENTS AND WISE DECISIONS

Eventually, adaptive action creates information that leads to decisions. Decision making in complex organizations is difficult enough when things are going well. During disruptive change—when, by definition, the environment is unstable and the way forward is unclear—decision making is even more of a challenge. For leaders, the stakes are high. Decisions made during times of disruptive change are defining moments; not only do they mark turning points for the organization, but they also crystallize the abilities of the leader for good or ill, in the minds of stakeholders. Wise decisions during times of crisis and change become part of the leader's legacy. Unwise decisions can destroy reputations.

Under ordinary conditions, educational leaders are expected to support strategic decisions through a process widely known as data-driven decision making (Marsh, Pane, & Hamilton, 2006). When leaders make decisions during disruptive change, however, data about what works in the new reality either does not exist or exists in nonrational forms or locations. In place of hard data, resilient leaders do not despair. They draw on information wherever they can, both in and out of the organization (Kaplan, 2012), including what they learn from trying things out, the counsel of important relationships in their network, wisdom from the field at large, and their own intuition.

As was described in the previous chapter, "Want Something More," the enduring elements of the organizational vision goes a long way to steer leaders toward the decisions they make. Where vision leaves off, however, gut feelings and intuition fill in. California Superintendent Patty Wool told me, "Resilience is more on the feeling level than the thinking level." Reflecting on a time early in her career when she was tasked by her superintendent to make unpopular schedule changes that would reduce extra-duty pay for some teachers—and do it on a short timeline—Wool reached an impasse that resisted rational argument. Wool told me, "The teachers were unwilling to support any change, and the superintendent still wanted something done."

In an oddly parallel situation, at the same time this challenge was unfolding in her workplace, Wool's cat climbed the highest tree in the neighborhood and became stuck. Unable or unwilling to climb back down, this cat stayed in the tree for several days and howled throughout the nights. Wool told me, "That cat's screaming across the neighborhood mirrored exactly what I was feeling inside." Wool remembers having the insight that she should call the area mountain climbing club and ask them to come over and get her cat out of the tree. Wool said, "Well, they came over and got the cat out of the tree, and that weekend I also knew what I was going to decide about the school schedule." Referring again to the intuitive nature of resilience, especially related to decision making, Wool adds, "When you get back in touch with the truth that you can figure things out in one area of your life, you see how you can figure anything out."

When the system is in commotion, leaders who do not listen to their gut feelings or lessons from other areas in their life miss out on a powerful source of information. For example, one high school principal I'll call "Joe" told me he regretted not listening to his gut feeling when the GPAs of several football players fell below the acceptable range and he had to respond. In the hullabaloo that followed, Joe wisely suspended the students from the game, but then he also decided *not* to provide them with the opportunity to receive extra academic support. "In retrospect, I was hardheaded," said Joe. "Even though my gut was telling me that 'the system' was also at fault, I thought the football players were not taking their classes seriously. The parents of these kids were really upset, and thc whole thing blew up at a board meeting. I was right in banning the athletes from the game, but if only I followed my gut and also made sure they had access to the academic support they needed, I would have been a better leader."

In the irreverent but uncanny distillation of enduring wisdom on the pratfalls of national defense, the brilliant Norman Augustine (1983) writes, "Ninety percent of the time things will turn out worse than you expect. The other ten percent of the time you had no right to expect so much" (p. 19). No matter what decisions a leader makes during times of disruptive change, they could be wrong. The corollary to this rule seems to be this: The higher the stakes and turbulence in the environment, the less perfect the decision. Bottom line, in every change there are both dangers and opportunities. Resiliency is seen in leaders who focus on the opportunities and leverage them in spite of the risk.

SUMMARY

Resilient leaders recognize that adversity brings opportunity—not the least of which is innovation that arises out of taking adaptive action. Adaptive action assumes that organizational learning is the goal, *not* perfection. Leaders who are reluctant to take action must deal with the fears that undermine their confidence. Once action is underway, leaders and their colleagues can begin to hone and refine the emerging innovations. Ultimately, what leaders learn from taking adaptive action allow them to make better decisions that help the organization bounce forward.

ACTIVITIES AND QUESTIONS FOR STUDY GROUPS AND TEAMS

1. With a particular challenge from your leadership work in mind, and as you reflect on the content in this chapter, what will you draw from the leadership resilience-enabling capacities of Relationships, Resonance, and Renewal, and how do you need to bolster them?

   The leadership challenge I'm thinking of is:

   In order to help myself and others Instigate Adaptive Action, I need to draw on these ideas from the three leadership resilience enablers:

   • Relationships:

   • Resonance:

   • Renewal:

2. What stories do you have about taking adaptive action in your life or work that you can share with others? What was the experiment? What did you revise, throw out, and keep? What were the key insights about taking adaptive action that you still think of today?

3. Does your culture support adaptive action? How do people in your school community feel about experiments and experiences on a small scale— where the outcome is uncertain but where the potential for learning about what works is high? How would you introduce the concept of adaptive action to your leaders or your school board?

4. What structures in your organization support or diminish the practice of adaptive action? For you? For others?

5. What are you aware of when you make decisions based on a large amount of intuition? What happens when you ignore your intuition? Tell your team about a time when either you ignored or listened to your intuition when making a decision.

6. What adaptive action is underway now in your organization? Who is trying
    out a strategy or initiative with the passionate intention to produce valuable
    results? Help the leaders of that experiment document their revisions for
    the next wave of participants. Take photos, record testimonials, gather and
    tell early impact "people stories," and support them in making presenta-
    tions and presenting their results.

11

Reflect & Celebrate

The hardness of life I deplore creates the qualities I admire.

—Florida Maxwell-Scott, 1968

Reminder: As you read this chapter, note where the ideas and strategies presented draw on the leadership resilience-enabling capacities of Relationships, Resonance, and Renewal. Then, at the end of the chapter, write down what you want to learn about or experience in order to bolster the capacities so that you are better able to respond in the aftermath of adversity and disruptive change.

Central to Leadership Resilience in Action is Reflect & Celebrate. At the same time, critical reflection is the process of becoming more aware about how we think, feel, and know ourselves, others, and the world around us. Celebration is a way to commemorate, honor, and admire not just what goes well, but what we learn from what does and doesn't go well.

PERSONAL REFLECTION AND CELEBRATION

Through critical reflection, resilience transforms into wisdom. In the aftermath of disruptive change, resilient leaders make countless passes through the process of reflection and celebration all within the context of uncertainty and conditions that sometimes defy existing assumptions. This is what the late Donald Schön (1983) describes when he bids professionals to move from technical rationality, where every problem has an answer, to "reflection in action," where professionals respond more intuitively to changing conditions with "artful competence" (p. 19). Of the many insights Schön provided to the fields of professional development and organizational learning, the idea that we all can reflect on what we are doing while we are doing it is profound. Schön, who was himself a jazz musician, compared reflection *in* action and reflection *on* action to playing in a jazz group improvising in response to the music. Schön says these musicians are "reflecting-in-action on the music they are collectively making and on their individual contributions to it, thinking what they are doing and, in the process evolving their way of doing it" (p. 56).

Meta Resilience

Resilient leaders become even more resilient by reflecting on their resiliency. In the midst of adversity, leaders who reflect-while-in-action not just about what happened and how they responded, but also *why* they responded the way they did and then improvise the next action, grow in wisdom about what it means to be resilient. Leaders who are undisciplined in reflective thinking tend to perceive only what they expect, through preexisting paradigms.

Michigan superintendent Mark Bielang makes a strong case for thinking about what you think and believe about your resilience. Bielang observed, "Being resilient almost happens intuitively; you have to take a step back afterward and understand the thinking behind your actions." According to Peter Senge (1990), leaders like Bielang elevate their mastery of resilience. Senge says, "What distinguishes people with high levels of personal mastery is that they have developed a higher level of rapport between their normal awareness and their subconscious. What most of us take for granted and exploit haphazardly, they approach as a discipline" (p. 162).

Consider the story of Jesse, a successful professor and administrator working in a prestigious university. Reflecting back on her late teens and early twenties recalling her headstrong nature to do exactly the opposite of whatever an authority figure told her to do, Jesse recalls being completely aware that she was making choices that were not always in her best interest. Back then, however, she did not know how to pull herself out of the strong emotions of anger, resentment, and powerlessness, and more often than not got herself involved in painful situations. She recalls thinking to herself, "What am I doing? What am I doing? I am messing up what could be my life." This repeated sequence in Jesse's youthful years created a strong emotional memory for her that serves her well today. When she feels those same emotions coming over her, she knows what they mean—and she now has the ability and wisdom to interrupt her habitual response and mindfully choose to respond more resonantly.

I admire Jesse more than I can say, for many leaders are trapped within what Chris Argyris (in Senge 1990) says are "defensive routines" that protect them from becoming aware of where they need to change and grow. Reflective leaders like Jesse have learned that powerful emotions draw their attention to opportunities for reflection. These leaders look around them and, like Jesse, ask themselves, "What am I doing here? Am I reacting in ways that makes the situation better or worse?"

PATHWAYS TO PERSONAL AND ORGANIZATIONAL REFLECTION AND CELEBRATION

While resilient leaders may choose different strategies for reflection, all highly resilient leaders are also highly reflective. Many strategies exist to promote reflection. In this section I summarize a few that I think are quite powerful and that I teach in my leadership development workshops. I encourage you to experiment with them and discover what works for you. One way to know if a reflective strategy is working for you is to notice if it empowers you to improvise and respond in ways that help you and the organization bounce forward.

Have a Thought Leadership Partner

A powerful way to make reflection a practice is to team up with a thought leadership partner. An example follows. Recently, an assistant superintendent of a school district in the Midwest asked me to provide him with a few consulting sessions to help him analyze the district student achievement data and put together a data presentation to the superintendent. During the previous month, the district accountability specialist quit, leaving my client, who I will call "Miles," with a thick stack of tables and graphs that showed a distinct absence of growth for the last six years but little coherence about what it all meant.

During one of our conversations, Miles sent me several charts showing longitudinal AYP (adequate yearly progress) data disaggregated for ethnicity and socioeconomic status. As with other data formats, it looked like the achievement gap had not changed one iota. Yet, both Hispanic and black students had increased enrollment in AP classes and decreased unexcused absences and expulsions. "Everyone is working really hard in my district," said Miles. "I just don't understand why we are not getting better as far as AYP goes." As I listened to Miles and looked at the district data, I thought it was possible that the AYP data was not sensitive enough to pick up subtle changes in growth or lack thereof. I expressed my theory to Miles saying, "I wonder what average scale scores would reveal about these achievement gaps?" That got Miles thinking. After our conversation, he went back to the data and did achievement gap calculations using scale scores. Although the data still showed persistent achievement gaps, the data also showed more specifically where small gains existed. This knowledge allowed Miles to work more precisely with specific schools and grade levels.

In this scenario, and during this conversation, I functioned for Miles as a thought leadership partner (Allison et al., 2012; Allison-Napolitano, 2013). Thought leadership partners are colleagues and coaches who think alongside of you, putting on the table for you to look at and chew over, the best of what is known in the field, about what you are facing. Thought leadership partners help us reflect by asking open-ended questions and bringing up theories, much more often than they give advice or share their own opinions. They introduce perspectives that are different from yours and that have the ability to jar your mind and challenge your cognitive distortions. And of course, thought leadership partners also just listen.

For Maggie Cuellar, an area superintendent in Texas, reflecting with a thought partner is different than reflecting alone. Cuellar told me, "When I can process and plan aloud, like I can in our coaching sessions, I think about things in a different way. Alone I think about what I have to do. With a thought partner I also think about what I am learning." Another leader, Mark Bielang, who was named Region VII Superintendent of the Year for 2012 by the Michigan Association of School Administrators, says, "I've had situations where I just need help in thinking something through. When I can't see past my blind spots, I talk with people who will ask me the right questions and give me another perspective. This happened recently when I had my mind made up about how to handle a grievance. Then, someone introduced a new way of thinking about it and I ended up totally changing my mind."

Showcase Small and Early Wins

Not only does focused action create momentum toward positive change in response to loss and challenge, but it also garners early wins (Watkins, 2003), which inspire confidence in supporters and doubters alike. Leaders who celebrate and broadcast early wins and small wins activate another approach to reflection not only for themselves, but for the entire organization. Any progress toward what you want more of, any movement toward achieving milestones, is worth noticing. As California superintendent Robert Haley told me, "Our goal has been to bring students who had previously decided to enroll in neighboring districts back to our schools. So far thirty students have returned. That might not sound like a lot, but thirty is more than zero!" When leaders celebrate and broadcast small and early wins, the effect goes beyond praising people and programs; it also informs and refines the next steps. This is as example of true reflection-in-action.

Small wins are anything you want more of: more teachers trained, more principals using new skills, more students engaged, more students graduating, and more students learning. For example, one teacher leader I know wanted to get students more engaged through questions. For one week, she asked students to give themselves a hash mark on a sticky note she put on their desk every time they asked a question about what they were learning. Increasing the number of questions asked by students may be a small win when it comes to increasing student engagement, but it is a small win in the right direction and on something that matters. One of the most important steps therefore in celebrating small wins is in knowing where they actually exist in the data and then setting up efficient systems to monitor their progress.

With a relentless focus on leveraging disruptive change to motivate toward the vision of the organization, small wins do not mean small goals. Harvard Business School researchers Teresa Amabile and Steven Kramer found that when it comes to change, small wins recognized regularly confirm for people that they are making progress on meaningful work (2011).

A Journal for Your "Favorite Mistakes"

With just a few moments of painful reflection, most of us can come up with several examples in our personal and professional lives when we really blew it. Perhaps we missed an opportunity, stayed in a bad relationship far too long, put our faith in someone who turned out to be unreliable, or we failed to follow through on a commitment. Although these blunders and poor calls make you wince when you think of them, most likely they also rendered powerful lessons that changed you and made you a little wiser. Favorite mistakes are those missteps where we learn the most.

One way to wring the maximum amount of learning out of your favorite mistakes is to keep a journal that lingers not on what actually went wrong, but on what you learned about yourself and about the system when it went wrong. The favorite mistakes journal is a tool that often leads to deep learning about how the organization actually prevents its own success. This type of learning is what Donald Schön and Chris Argyris, among others, refer to as double loop learning. Double loop learning means that you go beyond learning what doesn't work and then trying something different, to learning *that* something doesn't work and then looking deeper into structures in the system to learn how they help or hinder the situation. In double loop learning, the remedies, therefore, go beyond the surface from simply solving one problem to reengineering the underlying contributors to problems.

Leaders who reflect on and celebrate favorite mistakes do more than increase organizational learning: They also steer the culture toward accepting the idea that "mistakes" produce the most profound learning and ought to be mined for the pearls of wisdom they contain.

Hold a Learning Fair

In his book *Leading in a Culture of Change* (2001), Michael Fullan says, "If you remember one thing about information, it is that it only becomes valuable in a social context" (p. 78). Built on this idea, Fullan suggests holding a "learning fair," which provides a powerful social context for knowledge building and is an "opportunity to showcase, reflect and celebrate" (p. 101).

Knowledge building strategies such as the learning fair not only encourages reflection, but it also builds relationships. Fullan quotes Nancy Dixon, from her book *Common Knowledge,* who wrote, "If people begin sharing ideas about issues they see as really important, the sharing itself creates a learning culture" (in Fullan, 2001, p. 84).

Celebrate Cultural Shifts

When it comes to leveraging strengths and opportunities, resilient leaders never miss a chance to celebrate. Certainly, most leaders celebrate marked improvements in student achievement. But leaders that want to increase their resiliency and the resiliency of others do not wait to accomplish goals before they commemorate positive changes toward those goals. In addition, these leaders do not limit themselves to celebrating changes in student achievement; they also mark positive changes in organizational learning.

Organizational learning, a concept and term coined by Peter Senge in 1990, is seen when—through experience, collaboration, and reflection—individuals and teams contribute new insights to the organization that ultimately and fundamentally refine and reshape it. Savvy leaders pay attention to the process of organizational learning by celebrating changes in people and the culture that signify movement toward powerful practices. For example, school administrator Janine Hoke marks the increased number of faculty members who, after learning leadership coaching skills, ask each other more and better questions while in team meetings. Hoke says, "The better the questions, the better we are in engaging in conversations that get to the heart of vexing challenges. As a bonus, the results affirm to us that the practice of asking better questions is important. And so I celebrate it when I see it. Celebration reinforces good practice." Leaders like Hoke know that frequent and specific feedback about behaviors that pave the road to success is also a *strategy* for resilience.

iReflect-in-Action

As I mentioned in Chapter 5, I am a prolific recorder of memos to myself on my iPhone. The messages I send to myself contain my reflections and insights as they occur to me, usually when I am running or hiking but also while I work and interact with clients. As a method for reflection in action, your smartphone is an invaluable tool. For example, the novice principal named "Lee," whom you met in Chapter 8, is now using his smartphone to record a brief sentence or two about what he is thinking each time he either expresses a negative and skewed perspective or when he successfully recognized he was about to say something rash and unhelpful but stopped himself from doing so. Lee shares these recordings with his leadership coach, who helps him think out loud about what it means, what he can learn about himself, where he needs to make apologies, and what he needs to do in order to behave better the next time.

You can also use your smartphone to record a sentence or two that gives a teacher or colleague feedback about something they handled well or performed with artistry. Make the recording and simply e-mail it to the other person. Your feedback will mean a lot to them and will go far to bolster their resilience for the day.

SUMMARY

The cycle of leadership is incomplete without reflection and celebration. Reflection and celebration transform the lessons that come from leadership resilience into wisdom—for you, for the people you lead, and ultimately for the entire organization and profession. Keeping in line with what Florida Maxwell-Scott wrote in 1968 when she was well into her eighties, "The hardness of life I deplore creates the qualities I admire" (2013, p. 47), some of the best lessons come from what does *not* go well while you respond to adversity.

ACTIVITIES AND QUESTIONS FOR STUDY GROUPS AND TEAMS

1. With a particular challenge from your leadership work in mind, and as you reflect on the content in this chapter, what will you draw from the leadership resilience-enabling capacities of Relationships, Resonance, and Renewal, and how do you need to bolster them?

   The leadership challenge I'm thinking of is:

   In order to help myself and others Reflect & Celebrate, I need to draw on these ideas from the three leadership resilience enablers:

   • Relationships:

   • Resonance:

   • Renewal:

2. Try out one or more of the reflection-in-action strategies presented in this chapter, and share your reflections about how they worked for you with a leadership coach, colleague, or your team.

3. As a team, divide up the reflection-in-action strategies presented in this chapter and commit to using the one assigned to you each day for two weeks. Then, come back again as a team and teach the strategy assigned to you to your colleagues. Share what you learned about the strategy as well as yourself, and make suggestions for applying it further in your organization.

Part IV

Leading Organizational Resilience

12 Organizational Resilience Risks and Opportunities

Even the best leaders cannot predict a specific disruptive change or adverse incident. What they can do, however, is *shape* a resilient organization—an organization capable of responding to and bouncing forward from unpredictable events, no matter what form they take. This means that if you want to lead in an environment that supports, values, and enhances your leadership resilience and the resilience of others, you need to mindfully design and sustain a resilient organization. This chapter answers these questions: How will you know if your organizational resilience is at risk? How can you bring other leaders, board members, and stakeholders into the conversation and help them embrace the reality that adversity is neither unusual nor rare, and in fact, is essential to growth, relevancy, and sustainability? What are the actions you need to take to build an organization that sustains resilience?

BECOMING A RESILIENT ORGANIZATION

Resilience should not be an organization's emergency response, conjured up only in times of trouble. Resilient leaders and organizations accept the constant presence of loss and challenge and, therefore, they make *resilience* a personal and corporate value, and they mindfully sustain its defining qualities.

Figure Out If Something Is Fragile

Resilient leaders employ a tactic that proactively invites disorder into the system: They routinely scrutinize the organization for vulnerabilities—especially during times of apparent stability. In his book *Antifragile: Things That Gain From Disorder* (2012), Nassim Taleb applies ideas about the fragility and antifragility of financial markets to other complex systems. Taleb provocatively suggests that stability is like a time bomb—one that conceals vulnerabilities that ultimately makes a system fragile. Invoking the metaphor of a forest fire to explain this idea, Taleb writes, "the absence of fire lets highly flammable materials accumulate" (p. 105). Taleb's implication is clear: The inevitable fire will be devastating. Inviting disorder may sound like a crazy thing to do, but since adversity is neither rare nor unusual—and usually leads to insight and creativity—leaders who purposefully introduce disorder learn where vulnerabilities exist and how to strengthen the system. As Taleb advises, "It is far easier to figure out if something is fragile than to predict the occurrence of an event that may harm it" (Taleb, 2012, p. 4).

Conversations to Introduce Disorder

Resilient leaders don't wait for ticking time bombs to explode on their own; they purposefully set them off. They do this by starting conversations that bring vulnerabilities to the surface where they can be dealt with. These conversations invite disorder and therefore they may be uncomfortable—especially for those who subscribe to the "if it ain't broke don't fix it" philosophy. But they help leaders and their organizations get ahead of the effects of adversity and respond more innovatively, even though they cannot predict or stave off the adversity itself.

Authors of the book *The Innovator's DNA: Mastering the Five Skills of Disruptive Innovators* say that leaders become comfortable in the role of "disruptive innovator" by asking status-quo-challenging questions that explore key initiatives and uncover vulnerabilities in the way things are being done (Dyer et al., 2011). Asking status-quo-challenging questions is risky, of course, because they threaten those who are comfortable with the current state. Yet, resilient organizations sustain themselves only by being willing to change.

THE RESILIENCE RISK RUBRIC: A TOOL TO INTRODUCE INNOVATIVE DISRUPTION

The Resilience Risk Rubric is a tool for starting conversations where stakeholders take stock of key harbingers of non-resilience. These are the conditions—those "time bombs"—that alert you to a potential crack in the resilience of your organization. In this chapter, you'll have the opportunity to kick off these conversations in your organization by first using a rubric that alerts you to the level of current risk. Then, you can devise a plan of action to make your organization antifragile by moving it from its current state of resilience toward the exemplar.

The six risks we'll examine here are:

1. Top leaders have stopped learning.

2. We blame everything on the budget.

3. We ignore results on critical indicators.

4. We have too many unfocused initiatives, so now people say that they have "too much on their plate."

5. Success is uncelebrated.

6. We neglect our responsibility to develop leaders within our organization.

THE RESILIENCE RISK RUBRIC

The Resilience Risk Rubric presents the top six signs that an organization might be at risk of becoming "non-resilient." For each of the six resilience risks, use the exemplar provided as a point of reference to assess your level of risk. The *more* you or your organization resemble the exemplar, the *less* you are at risk for non-resilience. The *less* you or your organization resembles the exemplar, the *more* you are at risk for non-resilience.

Instructions

Step 1. For each of the six resilience risks, first read the summary that introduces the risk.

Step 2. After you read the summary, read through the bulleted exemplars, which describe the risk at its *least* vulnerable and therefore most desirable state. The exemplars flesh out an aspirational level of resilience for the risk. This is the level that you and your organization should aspire to achieve.

Step 3. After you read through the exemplars, rate your organization from 1–10, with 10 representing a direct match with the exemplar and with 1 representing the exact opposite of the exemplar.

Step 4. Compare your rating with other members of your team or organization and talk about the areas where the organization is vulnerable.

Step 5. Use the thought leadership questions (Allison et al., 2012), provided at the end of each section, to stimulate additional conversation within your leadership team and others.

Step 6. Decide what action you will take in order to move closer to the exemplars for each risk.

Resilience Risk 1: "Top Leaders Have Stopped Learning"

Summary: Learning is just another word for *change,* and as Peter Senge (1990) wrote, "Organizations learn only through individuals who learn" (p. 139). When things are going well, however, change is the last thing some leaders want to do, and so they skimp on learning. Especially when budgets are tight, professional development is often the first thing to go.

When top leaders in the organization quit learning, it means they believe they know everything they need to know. This is a form of hubris. Of course, organizations are dynamic; they are in a constant state of change, and leaders must continually learn about these changes. When top leaders in the organization quit learning, they put their resilience and the resilience of the organization at risk.

The Exemplar for "Not at Risk"

- I/We have a yearly learning agenda for each of the top initiatives in our organization. Our learning agenda includes opportunities to learn skills and processes for each initiative, and it includes learning experiences to build our understanding of systems, people, and theories of change.
- I/We engage in weekly events to learn about our top initiatives. Learning may involve analyzing performance data, attending professional development and training (on own and with others), attending book and article studies, and holding focus groups with stakeholders, shareholders, employees, suppliers, clients, or customers.
- I/We speak with front-line employees and stakeholders/customers/ clients every single day to gain their perspective about how our top initiatives are working.
- I/We identify key individuals whom we will coach and mentor into leadership roles for the top initiatives. These individuals engage in a minimum of twice-monthly coaching sessions and twice-monthly mentoring sessions.
- I/We identify one reflective question to illuminate each month, and we use it to analyze one or more of our top initiatives. These questions focus our inquiry and provide a framework for the insights we share with each other during our weekly learning agenda meetings.

How Vulnerable Is Your Organization for This Resilience Risk?

"The top leaders in my organization have stopped learning."

Your Rating

In serious risk			In moderate risk				Not at risk		
1	2	3	4	5	6	7	8	9	10

> ## THOUGHT LEADERSHIP QUESTIONS FOR RESILIENCE RISK 1: "TOP LEADERS HAVE STOPPED LEARNING"
>
> - What have we learned this week from employees on the front line of our initiatives?
> - What five questions will we illuminate about our initiatives this month?
> - Who are we mentoring or coaching to provide leadership in important initiatives?
> - What is our learning agenda each month? This year? What books will we read? What conferences will we attend? How will we use what we learned?

Resilience Risk 2: "We Blame Everything on the Budget"

Summary: Like time, money is finite. Every enterprise has a budget to match its mission, scope, and scale. Some organizations, especially those that use government funds and depend on local and state taxes and grants, make poor decisions when cash flow is strong. Here are just a few of the critical errors these organizations make: (1) they use soft money to fund important positions and programs (which are then cut when the money quits flowing), (2) they give money to the pet projects of certain people or groups (which they cannot get out of due to "politics"), (3) they don't monitor the added value of the initiatives they commit to and therefore do not make important revisions that keep them relevant and non-negotiable when hard times fall, and (4) they cut funding across the board without consideration for priorities and the greater good.

During times of economic fluctuation, non-resilient leaders make cuts across the board without regard for the mission and values of the organization. Or, they fail to challenge decisions to keep programs that no longer make sense. These individuals present themselves as victims of the economy and other forces out of their control. Their complaints focus on scarcity and signal a lack of resilience. They cut corners in important initiatives (such as professional development), which creates vulnerabilities in the system that will surface and undermine success when better economic times prevail. These leaders create anxiety, promote a scarcity mentality, and stifle innovation throughout the organization.

The Exemplar for "Not at Risk"

- Anyone can look at our budget and immediately know our priorities.
- When I/we talk about the budget between ourselves and with the larger group of stakeholders, shareholders, employees, the board, and clients/customers, we talk as much about our values and mission as we do about cash flow and payments due. Whether the economy is "good" or "bad," our budget always reflects our best work.

- I/We support innovative ideas that we evaluate for impact and consistency with our mission and values. *Innovation* does not mean we lose focus or pursue every new idea. In fact, often our innovations are incarnations and extensions of our best strategies, which maintain their relevancy in a changing world. These innovations ultimately strengthen our budget; they attract additional revenue.
- I/We sustain our best existing initiatives with support systems (professional development, coaching, talented workforce, leadership) that keep them vibrant and cutting edge. We know this is especially important during tough economic times. After all, why would we neglect our best and most focused work and then have to do double duty to restore and recover them?

How Vulnerable Is Your Organization for This Resilience Risk?

"The top leaders in the organization blame everything on the budget."

Your Rating

In serious risk			In moderate risk				Not at risk		
1	2	3	4	5	6	7	8	9	10

THOUGHT LEADERSHIP QUESTIONS FOR RESILIENCE RISK 2: "WE BLAME EVERYTHING ON THE BUDGET"

- What resources and support do our best initiatives need to succeed?
- What will we lose if we don't support our current initiative?
- What becomes possible if we made our current initiative strong and sustainable?
- If we don't support our current initiatives or any other great ideas now, how will we justify adding them back when our budget is stronger?
- What new initiatives will move our goals forward?
- How does our budget reflect our priorities?

Resilience Risk 3: "We Ignore Results on Critical Indicators"

Summary: Leaders need to know how each and every initiative in the enterprise is performing. Two or three key metrics, which provide essential feedback about how the organization is performing, need to be identified at the beginning of each initiative and for each strategy. Leading indicators can predict future trends, and although they are not always accurate, they certainly raise awareness and invite discussion and planning. When we look at them as information about the current reality that compels us to action toward the vision, updates in critical indicators are not to be feared but embraced for what they teach us. The discrepancies we discover in these data between what we want and what we currently have creates tension that ignites creativity.

Regular inspection of important metrics provides three benefits: (1) it maintains a sense of urgency and inspiration, (2) it inspires innovative responses and necessary refinements to strategies, and (3) it reveals victories that can be leveraged for greater returns.

Most leaders are keenly aware of the need to measure the "right" outputs, but not all leaders are as savvy as they believe themselves to be. When they do it right, leaders put structures in place to collect, analyze, report, and share important metrics *before* they implement initiatives.

The Exemplar for "Not at Risk"

- I/We know the indicators that track the success of each initiative in our organization. These indicators measure the impact of the strategy and their impact on the mission.
- I/We measure, analyze, discuss, share, and publish outcomes for each initiative on a regular schedule. Everyone is aware of the system we have in place to engage this process.
- People in all levels of our enterprise are aware of the indicators and the results our initiatives and strategies achieve. We use these data to refine and revise our approaches and to introduce adaptive action.
- Our organization looks at trend data. We understand that trends indicate the results we can continue to expect unless something changes. When we like the direction of the trend, we continue to renew and sustain the initiatives through innovation, acceleration, and support. When we dislike the direction of the trend, we seek to understand the facts and we take action to turn things around.
- When measuring progress toward student achievement goals, we disaggregate data into historically underserved groups including low income, limited English proficiency, students with IEPs, and minority groups.
- We look at data that allows us to view student achievement gaps and graduation gaps and how they have changed over the years.

How Vulnerable Is Your Organization for This Resilience Risk?

"I or the top leaders in my organization ignore results on critical indicators."

Your Rating

In serious risk			In moderate risk				Not at risk		
1	2	3	4	5	6	7	8	9	10

THOUGHT LEADERSHIP QUESTIONS FOR RESILIENCE RISK 3: "WE IGNORE RESULTS ON CRITICAL INDICATORS"

- Are we measuring outcomes that reflect the mission of our organization?
- What trends, even slight, do we see? What is the best we make of these trends? What is the worst we make of these trends?
- What else can the data mean?
- What assumptions does the data challenge?
- Who is impacted by the data? What stakeholder groups? What shareholder groups?

Resilience Risk 4: "We Have Too Many Unfocused Initiatives, So Now People Say That They Have 'Too Much on Their Plate'"

Summary: Ask almost any person working in any organization in any Western culture how they are doing, and they will answer with the words, "I'm very busy." In my leadership and coaching workshops, "busyness" is the number one excuse people give for not getting to the most important work on their plate. Ironically, trivial time wasters and "fires" that need putting out today undermine high-leverage action and therefore actually create the crisis situations of tomorrow. In their *Harvard Business Review* article (2010), Bruch and Menges refer to this sense of overload as the "acceleration trap." According to Bruch and Menges, organizations caught in the acceleration trap overload people without giving them a break, multiload the system with too many different activities, and continually load the system with new initiatives without unloading old ones.

Leaders need to take the lead; they need to quit talking about how busy they are and instead take control of their ability to design and focus on work that matters. Bottom line, a sense of powerlessness is the subtext behind complaints of being too busy. Leaders who find themselves and others talking about how busy they are need to take control of their priorities.

The Exemplar for "Not at Risk"

- I/We do work that has meaning. Therefore, even though we are quite engaged throughout the day, we are energized—not "busy."
- I/We can name all of our high-impact initiatives and strategies, and we use more time and energy focusing on these initiatives than we do on tasks from a low-level "to do" list.
- I/We renew and revise our high-impact initiatives. We keep them sharp and relevant. Instead of constantly overloading the system with "new" initiatives, we concentrate on bringing our best work to full implementation. This is not to say that we are not innovative. This is to say that we continue to innovate within our best initiatives, and we remain focused on our mission.
- I/We build in cycles of renewal for people in order to break the "busy" trap and to create and sustain energy for the most important work we do.
- I/We do not talk about how busy we are. Instead, we describe our work and how it makes a difference. We manage requests that other people make of us, and therefore do not blame others for how we use our time and energy.
- I/We have processes for terminating non-essential tasks and for using data in order to understand where our best work needs concentrated attention, management, revision, and innovation.

How Vulnerable Is Your Organization for This Resilience Risk?

"We have too many unfocused initiatives, so now people say that they have 'too much on their plate.'"

Your Rating

In serious risk			In moderate risk				Not at risk		
1	2	3	4	5	6	7	8	9	10

THOUGHT LEADERSHIP QUESTIONS FOR RESILIENCE RISK 4: "WE HAVE TOO MANY UNFOCUSED INITIATIVES, SO NOW PEOPLE SAY THAT THEY HAVE 'TOO MUCH ON THEIR PLATE'"

- What do people in this organization say is our most important work? What percentage of their energy and time goes into this work?
- What are we not getting to that troubles us most?
- What will be our legacy?
- How do we sustain organizational energy?
- How do we promote a culture of renewal?

Resilience Risk 5: "Success Is Uncelebrated"

Summary: Great leaders do not celebrate success in a Pollyanna effort to make everyone feel better or as a reason to put a cake in the staff room (though there's nothing wrong with cake!). No, they celebrate success in order to understand what individuals and the system itself does to create success. During times of strife, it is easy to succumb to negative emotional force fields in the system, which are characterized more by fear than inspiration. What's going "right" in the organization is overshadowed by what's going "wrong." The real loss, when this happens, is the opportunity to provide feedback that leads to learning, which could very possibly provide the breakthrough needed to alter the current challenge.

Exemplar for "Not at Risk"

- I/We look for small wins (anything that is more of what you want) in multiple places in the system.
- I/We have multiple venues for broadcasting wins (newsletters, websites, meetings, presentations, in person), and we use them in planned intervals and spontaneously when the wins occur.
- I/We celebrate wins and success achieved by all stakeholder, shareholder, client, customer, and partner groups in the system.
- I/We dialogue about the "wins," asking questions like: What was the turning point? What could jeopardize our approaches? What does this win now make possible? We use the insights that come from these dialogues to advance our strategies.

How Vulnerable Is Your Organization for This Resilience Risk?
"Success is uncelebrated."

Your Rating

In serious risk			In moderate risk				Not at risk		
1	2	3	4	5	6	7	8	9	10

THOUGHT LEADERSHIP QUESTIONS FOR RESILIENCE RISK 5: "SUCCESS IS UNCELEBRATED"

- What counts as "early wins" in our top three initiatives?
- How do we assure that everyone in the organization knows our current status relative to our desired status?
- How do we use or misuse successes to encourage or discourage people?
- What do we want more of?
- What is worth celebrating in our organization?

Resilience Risk 6: "We Neglect Our Responsibility to Develop Leaders Within Our Organization"

Summary: In a review of research commissioned by the Wallace Foundation (Leithwood, Seashore Louis, Anderson, & Wahlstom, 2004) about how leadership influences student learning, the authors write that especially in underperforming schools, "Leadership is second only to classroom instruction among all school related factors that contribute to what students learn at schools" (p. 5). The authors summarize the core practices of good leadership as the ability to set direction, develop people, and redesign structures in the organization to support rather than hinder successful practices. Given the powerful impact leadership has on learning, resilient organizations make leadership development a strategic priority.

The Exemplar for "Not at Risk"

- Our budget secures and preserves financial support and resources for leadership development.
- We have a plan for identifying promising leaders, and we are transparent about our recruitment and hiring process and the qualities of leadership needed.
- Our leadership education program and the professional development partners we team with strategically focus on the goals of our organization informed by aspirational leadership standards in education.
- Our leadership development program focuses on authentic contexts where theory comes to life in practice through coaching, job shadowing, job sharing, internships, and mentoring programs that pair aspiring leaders with resonant and reflective practitioners.
- Senior leaders in our organization recognize that developing other leaders is a priority responsibility, and they personally engage in activities each week that demonstrate a long-term investment in people.
- Our culture favors transformational leadership of instruction and curriculum over short-term gains and management of the status quo.
- In our organization we celebrate the value of learning as much as we celebrate the outcomes of our efforts.
- We encourage aspiring and current leaders to take the helm of projects that draw on their passions and that move the goals of the organization forward in authentic "nitty-gritty" contexts.
- Our organization has brought leadership coaching and mentoring to scale. Aspiring and veteran leaders alike have access to coaching, and our leaders have learned leadership coaching and mentoring skills, which they skillfully apply on the job to support aspiring and new leaders and their veteran colleagues.

- We have a leadership feedback and evaluation system that links to aspirational leadership standards, and we provide support to help leaders become better.
- Our leaders set an example of lifelong learning, and they are transparent about their own need to learn. On the job, they ask other people to teach them.

How Vulnerable Is Your Organization for This Resilience Risk?

"We neglect our responsibility to develop leaders within our organization."

Your Rating

In serious risk			In moderate risk				Not at risk		
1	2	3	4	5	6	7	8	9	10

THOUGHT LEADERSHIP QUESTIONS FOR RESILIENCE RISK 6: "WE NEGLECT OUR RESPONSIBILITY TO DEVELOP LEADERS WITHIN OUR ORGANIZATION"

- What are we learning? What are we teaching others these days?
- Which of the goals in our organization have to do with developing people?
- What is our organizational capacity for leadership coaching and mentoring?
- How open are we about supporting the passions of aspiring and current leaders?
- If our organization was really great at developing leadership in others, what would we gain?

13 A Final Word

Forgive Yourself
Every Day

Finish each day and be done with it. You have done what you could; some blunders and absurdities have crept in; forget them as soon as you can. Tomorrow is a new day; you shall begin it serenely and with too high a spirit to be encumbered with your old nonsense.

—Ralph Waldo Emerson

In 2000 I began a disciplined study on the nature of wisdom. Due to the semantic conundrums surrounding even the most basic definitions of wisdom, people within the academic wisdom circles I traffic commonly joke that only a fool would consider studying it. Perhaps this explains why I earnestly pursued the topic, eventually earning a doctorate for my dissertation on the nature of wisdom in nurses. As a true wisdom geek, I continued to interview wise people, from all walks of life, even after I earned my degree. In 2007 I had the great privilege of interviewing Teresa McCoy, a leader in the Eastern Band of the Cherokee Nation, who was also known for her wisdom. I asked Teresa to tell me about love. She said, "No matter what you love—your nation, your community, the organization you lead, your family, or another person—you must wake up every morning and forgive yourself for whatever is bothering you. This is how you make room for the challenges of the new day."

Teresa's words echo the essential and potent messages of virtually every leader I interviewed while writing this book: You must care deeply and show up every day, inspired and confident that you can and will make a difference. You must tenderly forgive yourself for your blunders and foibles—for your humanness. This above all other strategies will allow you to bounce forward and continue your work for a greater good.

Appendix

Films, Music, and Literature to Conjure Up Ideas About Leadership Resilience

This is a partial list of the "right brain" prompts that cause me to think about leadership resilience. Although I've watched all these films, listen regularly to this music, and have read these books and poems more than once, every time I come back to them I learn something new about what it means to be resilient and what it means to be a resilient leader. I provide you with this list with the hope that as individuals and as teams, you will take time to indulge in them—experience them either alone or together and notice the insights you have about leadership resilience in your life and in your work.

FILMS

Look beyond the obvious messages in these films and try to ignore the clichés. Think about the leadership resilience-enabling capacities of Relationships, Resonance, and Renewal as you watch. Which characters exemplify the best of leadership resilience? What story arcs show the transformation in characters who face adversity and eventually come out ahead?

1. *Castaway*

2. *Napoleon Dynamite*

3. *Late Bloomers*

4. *Schindler's List*

5. *Stand By Me*

   6. *Little Miss Sunshine*

   7. *Muriel's Wedding*

   8. *Apocalypse Now*

   9. *In Harm's Way* (John Wayne)

 10. *Fargo*

 11. *O Brother, Where Art Thou?*

 12. *Hope Floats*

 13. *Remember the Titans*

 14. *The Green Mile*

 15. *The Shawshank Redemption*

 16. *Precious*

 17. *Hotel Rwanda*

 18. *Shrek*

MUSIC

Suggestion: Make yourself a playlist of songs that strengthen you. Select one or more as your personal theme song (à la Ally McBeal) and play it in the morning or when you are exercising or taking a micro-break during a demanding day.

   1. "Beautiful Day" by U2 (You have to get the disco version!)

   2. "Stuck in a Moment" by U2

   3. "Singin' in the Rain"

   4. "I Can See Clearly Now"

   5. "Don't Stop Believing" (*Glee* cover)

   6. "Don't Stop Thinking About Tomorrow"

   7. "Back in the High Life Again"

   8. "You Raise Me Up" (Josh Groban)

   9. "Gimme Hope" (Eddy Grant)

 10. "Here" (Mariah Carey)

 11. "Stand by Me" by any artist (submitted by Bonnie Bishop)

12. "At Last" by Etta James (submitted by Bonnie Bishop)

13. "Shower the People" by James Taylor (submitted by Bonnie Bishop)

LITERATURE AND POETRY

1. *Teaching a Stone to Talk: Expeditions and Encounters* by Annie Dillard. Especially the quote: "But as she has grown, her smile had widened with a touch of feat and her glance has taken on depth. Now she is aware of some of the losses you incur by being here—the extraordinary rent you have to pay as long as you stay."

2. *The Journey* (poem by Mary Oliver)

3. *As I Lay Dying*

4. *On the Origin of Species* by Charles Darwin

5. *Band of Brothers*

6. *Life of Pi*

7. *The Pearl*

8. *Grapes of Wrath*

References

Allison, E. (2011). On the job stress busters. Retrieved from http://wisdomout.com/wp-content/uploads/2012/02/On-the-job-stress-busters2.pdf

Allison, E., & Reeves, D. (2012). *Renewal coaching fieldbook: How effective leaders sustain meaningful change.* San Francisco, CA: Jossey-Bass.

Allison-Napolitano, E. (2011, May 25). Stare back at fear: 25 things leaders can do everyday. Retrieved from http://wisdomout.com/stare-back-at-fear-25-things-leaders-can-do-everyday/

Allison-Napolitano, E. (2013). *Flywheel: Transformational leadership coaching for sustainable change.* Thousand Oaks, CA: Corwin.

Amabile, T. M., & Kramer, S. J. (2011). *The progress principal: Using small wins to ignite joy, engagement, and creativity at work.* Cambridge, MA: Harvard Business Review Press.

American Psychological Association (APA). (2002). The road to resilience. Retrieved from http://www.apa.org/helpcenter/road-resilience.aspx

Ariely, D. (2010). *Predictably irrational: The hidden forces that shape our destiny.* New York, NY: Harper Perennial.

Ariely, D. (2010, January). The long term effects of short-term emotions. *Harvard Business Review.*

Augustine, N. R. (1983). *Augustine's laws: Revised and enlarged.* New York, NY: American Institute of Aeronautics and Astronautics.

Baber, A., & Waymon, L. (2007). *Make your contacts count: Networking know-how for business and career success.* New York, NY: AMCOM, American Management Association.

Blackburn, E. H. (2009, November). Nobel Lecture: *Telomeres and telomerase: The means to the end.* Nobelprize.org. Nobel Media AB 2013. Web. 14. Retrieved from http://www.nobelprize.org/nobel_prizes/medicine/laureates/2009/blackburn-lecture.html

Block, J. H., & Block, J. (1980). The role of ego-control and ego-resiliency in the organization of behavior. In W. A. Collins (Ed.), *Development of cognition, affect, and social relations: Minnesota Symposia on Child Psychology* (Vol. 13, pp. 39–101). Hillsdale, NJ: Erlbaum.

Bonanno, G. A. (2009). *The other side of sadness: What the new science of bereavement tells us about life after loss.* New York, NY: Basic Books.

Bonanno, G. A., Galea, S., Bucciareli, A., & Vlahov, D. (2007). What predicts psychological resilience after disaster? The role of demographics, resources, and life stress. *Journal of Consulting and Clinical Psychology, 75*(5), 671–682.

Box, George E. P., & Draper, N. R. (1987). *Empirical model-building and response surfaces* (p. 424). San Francisco, CA: Wiley.

Boyatzis, R. E., & McKee, A. (2005). *Resonant leadership: Renewing yourself and connecting with others through mindfulness, hope, and compassion.* Boston, MA: Harvard Business School Press.

Bridges, W. (1980). *Transitions.* New York, NY: Addison-Wesley.

Brown-Easton, L. (2008). *Powerful designs for professional learning* (2nd ed.). Oxford, OH: National Staff Development Council.

Bruch, H., & Menges, J. I. (2010, April). The acceleration trap. *Harvard Business Review.*

Butler, L. D., Blasey, C. M., Garlan, R. W., McCaslin, S. E., Azarow, J., Chen, X.-H., . . . Spiegel, D. (2005). Posttraumatic growth following the terrorist attacks of September 11, 2001: Cognitive, coping, and trauma symptoms predictors in an Internet convenience sample. *Traumatology, 11,* 247–267.

Cacioppo, J. T., & Patrick, W. (2008). *Loneliness: Human nature and the need for social connection.* Boston, MA: Tantor Media.

Calhoun, L. G., & Tedeschi, R. G. (2006). *The handbook of posttraumatic growth: Research and practice.* Mahwah, NJ: Lawrence Erlbaum Associates.

Caruso, D. R., & Salovey, P. (2004). *The emotionally intelligent manager.* San Francisco, CA: Jossey-Bass.

Clay, R., Knibbs, J., & Joseph, S. (2009). Measurement of posttraumatic growth in young people: A review. *Clinical Child Psychology & Psychiatry, 14*(3), 411–422.

Davidson, R. J. (2012). *The emotional life of your brain: How its unique patterns affect the way you think, feel, and live—and how you can change them.* New York, NY: Hudson Street Press.

Davidson, R., Kabat-Zinn, J., Schumacher, J., Rosenkranz, M., Muller, D., Santorelli, S. F., . . . Sheridan, J. F. (2003). Alterations in brain and immune function produced by mindfulness meditation. *Psychosomatic Medicine, 65,* 564–570.

de Lange, T., Lundblad, V., & Blackburn, E. (2006). *Telomeres* (2nd ed.). USA: Cold Spring Harbor Laboratory Press.

Dyer, J., Gregersen, H., & Christensen, C. M. (2011). *The innovator's DNA: Mastering the five skills of disruptive innovators* [Kindle edition]. Perseus Books Group.

Epel, E. S., Blackburn, E. H., Lin, J., Dhabner, F. S., Adler, N. E., Morrow, J. D. et al. (2004). Accelerated telomere shortening in response to life stress. *Proceedings of the National Academy of Sciences, 101,* 17312–17315.

Fritz, C. (May 2012). Coffee breaks don't boost productivity after all. Cambridge, MA: *Harvard Business Review.*

Fullan, M. (1993). *Change force: Probing the depths of education reform.* London: The Falmer Press.

Fullan, M. (2001). *Leading in a culture of change.* San Francisco, CA: Jossey-Bass.

Fullan, M. (2008). *The six secrets of change: What the best leaders do to help their organizations survive and thrive.* San Francisco, CA: Jossey-Bass.

Ginsberg, R., & Multon, K. D. (2011). Leading through a fiscal nightmare: The impact on principals and superintendents. *Kappan, 92*(8), 42–47.

Goldstein, A. N., Greer, S. M., Saletin, J. M., Harvey, A. G., Nitschke, J. B., & Walker, M. P. (2013, June 26). Tired and apprehensive: Anxiety amplifies the impact of sleep loss on aversive brain anticipation. *The Journal of Neuroscience, 33*(26), 10607–10615. doi:10. 1523/JNEUROSCI. 5578–12. 2013

Goleman, D. (1998). *Working with emotional intelligence.* New York, NY: Bantam Books.

Goleman, D. (2004). *Destructive emotions. How can we overcome them? A scientific dialogue with the Dalai Lama.* New York, NY: Bantam Books.

Goleman, D. (2011). *The brain and emotional intelligence: New insights* [Kindle edition]. Northampton, MA: More Than Sound.

Goleman, D., Boyatzis, R., & McKee, A. (2004). *Primal leadership: Realizing the power of emotional intelligence.* Boston, MA: Harvard Business School Press.

Grady, V. M., & Grady, J. D. (2012). *The pivot point: Success in organizational change.* New York, NY: Morgan James Publishing

Hamel, G. (2009). Moonshots for management. *Harvard Business Review, 8*(10), 1–9.

Harland, L., Harrison, W., Jones, J., & Reiter-Palmon, R. (2005, Winter). Leadership behaviors and subordinate resilience. *Journal of Leadership and Organizational Studies, 11,* 2–14.

Ibarra, H., & Hunter, M. (2007). How leaders create and use networks. In *Harvard Business Review on the tests of a leader.* Cambridge, MA: Harvard Business School Press.

Isaacs, W. (1999). *Dialogue and the art of thinking together: A pioneering approach to communicating in business and life.* New York, NY: Doubleday.

Jetten, J., Haslam, C., Haslam, S. A., & Branscombe, N. R. (2009, September). The social cure. *Scientific American Mind, 20,* 26–33.

Johnson, S. (2010). *Where good ideas come from: The natural history of innovation.* New York, NY: Riverhead Books.

Kaplan, S. (2012). *Leapfrogging: Harness the power of surprise for business break-throughs.* San Francisco, CA: Berrett-Koehler.

Knoke, D. 1999. Organizational networks and corporate social capital. In S. M. Gabbay (Ed.), *Corporate social capital and liability* (pp. 17–42). Boston, MA: Kluwer.

Kobasa, S. C. (1979). Stressful life events, personality, and health—Inquiry into hardiness. *Journal of Personality and Social Psychology, 37,* 1–11.

Leithwood, K., Seashore Louis, K., Anderson, S., & Wahlstom, K. (2004). *How leadership influences student learning.* New York, NY: Wallace Foundation.

Lynch, J. (2000). *A cry unheard: New insights into the medical consequences of loneliness.* Baltimore, MD: Bancroft Press.

Marsh, J. A., Pane, J. F., & Hamilton, L. S. (2006). *Making sense of data-driven decision making in education; Evidence from recent Rand research.* Santa Monica, CA: Rand.

Maxwell-Scott, F. (2013). *The measure of my days: One woman's vivid, enduring celebration of life and learning.* New York, NY: Penguin Books.

McKee, A., Johnston, F., & Massimilian, R. (2006, May/June). Mindfulness, hope and compassion: A leader's road map to renewal. *Ivey Business Journal: Improving the Practice of Management.* Reprint # 9B06TC04. Ivey Management Services: The University of Western Ontario, London, Ontario. Retrieved from http://iveybusinessjournal.com/topics/leadership/mindfulness-hope-and-compassion-a-leaders-road-map-to-renewal#.UrRu2xzw2CY

Merchant, N. (2013, January 14). Sitting is the smoking of our generation. *Harvard Business Review* Blog Network. Retrieved from http://blogs.hbr.org/2013/01/sitting-is-the-smoking-of-our-generation/

Mezirow, J. (2000). Learning to think as an adult: Core concepts of transformation theory. In Mezirow and Associates (Eds.), *Learning as transformation* (pp. 3–34). San Francisco, CA: Jossey-Bass.

Nahapiet, J., & Ghoshal, S. (1998). Social capital, intellectual capital, and the organizational advantage. *Academy of Management Review, 23,* 242.

Nichols, M. (1995). *The lost art of listening: How learning to listen can improve relationships.* NY: The Guilford Press.

O'Brien, J. (2011, April 4). Exercise may prevent impact of stress on telomeres, a measure of cell health. University of California San Francisco online newsletter http://www.ucsf.edu/news/2011/04/9652/exercise-may-prevent-impact-stress-telomeres-measure-cell-health

Ozbay, F., Johnson, D., Dimoulas, E., Morgan, C., Charney, D., & Southwick, S. (2007, May). Social support and resilience to stress: From neurobiology to clinical practice. *Psychiatry,* 35–40.

Peters, T. (2001). Rule #3: Leadership is confusing as hell. *Fast Company.* Retrieved from http://www.fastcompany.com/magazine/44/march-2001

Pink, D. (2009). *Drive: The surprising truth about what motivates us.* New York, NY: Riverhead Books.

Putnam, R. D. (2000). *Bowling alone: The collapse and revival of American community.* San Francisco, CA: Simon-Schuster.

Reivich, K., & Shatté, A. (2002). *The resilience factor: Seven essential skills for overcoming life's inevitable obstacles* [Kindle edition]. Random House.

Sanders, T. (2002). *Love is the killer app: How to win business and influence friends.* New York, NY: Three Rivers Press.

Sapolsky, R. (2004). *Why zebras don't get ulcers: An updated guide to stress, stress-related diseases, and coping* (3rd ed.). New York, NY: Henry Holt & Co.

Scales, P. C., Benson, P. L., Leffert, N., & Blyth, D. A. (2000). Contribution of developmental assets to the prediction of thriving among adolescents. *Applied Developmental Science, 4*(1), 27–46.

Schön, D. A. (1983). *The reflective practitioner. How professionals think in action.* London, United Kingdom: Temple Smith.

Seligman, M. (1991). *Learned optimism: How to change your mind and your life* (2nd ed.). New York, NY: Simon and Schuster.

Seligman, M. (2011a). *Flourish: A visionary new understanding of happiness and well-being.* New York, NY: Free Press.

Seligman, M. (2011b, April). Building resilience. *Harvard Business Review.*

Senge, P. M. (1990). *The fifth discipline: The art and practice of the learning organization.* New York, NY: Doubleday.

Siebert, A. (2005). *The resiliency advantage: Master change, thrive under pressure, and bounce back from setbacks.* San Francisco, CA: Berrett-Koehler.

Singer, T. (2011). S*tress less (for women): Calm your body, slow aging, and rejuvenate the mind in 5 simple steps.* New York, NY: Hudson Street Press.

Sutton, R. I. (2008, August 13). Are you being a jerk? Again? Bloomberg *Businessweek.* Retrieved from http://www.businessweek.com/stories/2008-08-13/are-you-being-a-jerk-again

Taleb, N. (2012). *Antifragility: Things that gain from disorder*. New York, NY: Random House.

Tedeschi, R. G., & Calhoun, L. G. (1995). *Trauma and transformation: Growing in the aftermath of suffering*. Thousand Oaks, CA: Sage.

Tedeschi, R. G., & Calhoun, L. G. (2004). *Posttraumatic growth: Conceptual foundation and empirical evidence*. Philadelphia, PA: Lawrence Erlbaum Associates.

Tedlow, R. S. (2010). *Denial: Why business leaders fail to look facts in the face—and what to do about it*. New York, NY: Penguin Group.

Towers and Perrin. (2007). Engaged versus disengaged: The Gallup Organization, http://www.gallup.com/consulting/52/employee-engagement.aspx

Watkins, M. D. (2003). *The first 90 days: Critical success strategies for new leaders at all levels*. Boston, MA: Harvard Business School Publishing.

Wineapple, B. (2009). *White heat: The friendship of Emily Dickinson and Thomas Wentworth Higginson*. New York, NY: Anchor Books.

von Oech, R. (1990). *A whack on the side of the head: How you can be more creative* (revised). New York, NY: Warner Books.

Zautra, A. J., Hall, J. S., & Murray, K. E. (2010). Resilience: A new definition of health for people and communities. In J. W. Reich, A. J. Zautra, & J. S. Hall (Eds.), *Handbook of adult resilience* (pp. 3–34). New York, NY: Guilford.

Zolli, A., & Healy, A. M. (2012). *Resilience* [Kindle edition]. Simon & Schuster.

Index